# GO

# FOR

# FREE!

# GO FOR FREE!

The Complete Guide To
Free and Discount
Vacations

by     Dennis P. Sheridan

VENTONE PUBLISHING
Merrick, New York

Library of Congress Catalog Card Number 88-93100
ISBN 0-924337-00-1

Printed in The United States Of America

Ventone Publishing
P.O. Box 100
Merrick, NY 11566

*To Sharon, Joe and Mom*

# CONTENTS

# INTRODUCTION

Have you ever wondered how some friends, relatives, fellow workers or neighbors have been able to take glamorous vacations every year to places like Hawaii, Europe, Florida or California? Have you only been able to afford a short vacation or have you just stayed home - because you couldn't afford the cost of airline tickets, hotel rooms and car rentals? Some people take their vacations and don't worry about the costs involved. It's also possible that some of these people know about the secrets of free travel which they are not sharing with you.

Now, it's possible for YOU to enjoy a luxury vacation every year. The secrets of free travel will no longer be a mystery now that you have this book in your hands. With a minimum of effort on your part, and using the suggestions found here, you will become the envy of those you know, and you will enjoy the vacation of your dreams. And better still, you can GO FOR FREE!

Statistics provided by the United States Department of Transportation and by the airlines indicate that in 1988, approximately 475 million people travelled by air. What the government does not report, nor do the airlines want to broadcast, is that almost 1,000,000 people traveled for free. You too can be one of the chosen few who can fly for free or for next to nothing.

## Purpose

This book was written for only one purpose: To save you money when you travel. It's no secret that your vacation cost may be one of the largest expenses you will incur each year. This book will show you how to take MAXIMUM advantage of reduced airline fares. It will teach you many tricks for reducing your vacation costs. Most importantly, it will show you how to obtain free tickets from the airlines and free hotel rooms from the major hotel chains.

There have been many articles and books written about free vacations which suggest that you become a travel agent or that you go to work for an airline. Others have suggested that you work your way around the world on a tramp steamer, or that you arrange group trips and earn your own free travel. These are great ideas for people who are willing to change their life style or who have lots of spare time on their hands. The cost saving ideas in this book will not require you to change your life in any respect. You will not have to spend your spare time working or selling. You can actually accomplish most of the cost saving suggestions in this book from within the comfort of your own home.

The information in this book is intended for the average person who would like to take a well-deserved vacation every once in a while and save money doing it. You will learn how to find the best vacation bargains. Just because you are looking for an inexpensive vacation does not mean that you have to accept second rate service or inferior accommodations. A bargain priced vacation can be a value packed vacation. You will also learn how to obtain free airline tickets, free hotel rooms and free car rentals. Nothing is more satisfying than a vacation when you GO FOR FREE!

Last year, using the advice in this book, a couple in Houston flew to Hawaii for free. They stayed at a luxurious resort for only 50% of the standard rate, and enjoyed the vacation of their dreams! They enjoyed this so much, they recently spent a weekend at an Orlando resort for free and brought another couple along with them as well! They are now working on their next free trip to New York.

If you follow the advice in this book carefully, you can easily save 100's or 1000's of dollars on your next vacation. With a little determination, you can obtain your own free airline tickets and be on the way to your free vacation.

## How To Use This Book

You have already taken the most important step toward saving money on your next vacation - reading this book. If you are like most people, you cannot afford to go on a luxury vacation very often, if ever. Chances are pretty good that if you have taken a trip in the last year or so, you are quite aware that these costs are rising astronomically. The more you learn about airlines, hotels and travel promotions, the better prepared you will be. Armed with the knowledge in this book, you will be able to sort through all the confusion, and cut your vacation costs significantly.

There is a tremendous wealth of information in the pages that follow. Most of it has never been published in one place before. There are more than 100 money saving ideas or suggestions which you can use. You might not be able to use every money saving tip included. There will be times when you will be able to use some of these ideas for a short weekend getaway. Others suggestions will be perfect for your annual two week holiday. If one suggestion does not work for you, try another. Depending on your personal situation, you might be able to use 3 or 4 ideas at the same time, saving even more than you ever expected. Whenever possible, tips for doubling up on money saving plans have been included.

Read through this book once to get a good feel for the various cost savings plans. Then, reread it carefully and select the plan or plans which will work best for you. It is strongly recommended that you try each one. You might want to read through the book a third time to make certain that you thoroughly understand the steps you should follow, and to make sure you have not forgotten anything. Be sure to take notes, and when you are ready to begin saving money, follow these plans step by step.

## What To Expect

There are very few things in life which come to you without some effort on your part. You have probably heard the expression "there's no such thing as a free lunch." This is very true. Airlines and hotels do not beat a path to your door with free tickets or huge discounts. There will be a limited amount of effort required on your part in order to save money. You will soon find out how to have the airlines and hotels advise you of these bargains. They may not beat a path to your door, but they will certainly flood your mailbox with this information.

If you follow the advice in these pages, then the next time you travel, whether alone or with your family or companions, whether in one week's time or next year, you should be able to save a substantial amount of money - or even GO FOR FREE!

# ALL
# ABOUT
# VACATIONS

It is essential that you understand what is happening in the world of travel, how airlines and hotels operate, and how they set their rates. Understanding the rules of the travel game will allow you as a player not only to take advantage of the system, but to also play much more professionally.

## The Phases Of A Vacation

There are 3 basic phases to every vacation - planning, enjoying and reflecting. This book is basically concerned with the planning phase. It will not help you enjoy yourself when you arrive at your destination - with one possible exception - knowing that you have saved a bundle getting there! You have to supply the element of excitement, quiet, splendor or sentiment yourself.

This book is not concerned with the reflecting phase. You will have to take the time to think back about the good times that were enjoyed, the peace and quiet, or the beauty of places you visited. Only you can enjoy the photographs, souvenirs, and memories. The only advice that can be offered for your reflections about your trip is that you should have saved enough money to start planning your next one!

## The Fundamentals Of A Vacation

There are 4 fundamental elements which go in to almost every vacation - transportation, lodging, food and spending money. This is true whether you are taking the family to the mountains in your own car, or if you are taking a once-in-a-lifetime trip to Europe or Hawaii. Transportation and lodging have been, without doubt, the biggest chunk of your vacation budget in the past. This book will concentrate on saving you money on these two items.

## Transportation

Transportation includes airlines, railroads, buses, car rentals or the use of your own automobile. This book will concentrate on everyone's favorite means of getting to that distant location - the airlines. If you decide to rent a car for your trip or if you wish to take a cruise, you can learn how to obtain these with large discounts or even GO FOR FREE! - so read on. If you drive a car to your vacation destination, the information in this book will be of great value to you in respect to your lodging expenses. You may even learn how to obtain the free use of a car - so don't despair.

Most modern travelers have avoided buses and railroads because of their inconvenience, but mostly because a plane can get them to their destination in a fraction of the time. If you prefer buses or trains, make sure you read the tips suggested for getting the best rate from an airline, covered in Chapter 4. Try them with the railroad or bus lines; they very often work.

## Lodging

Lodging includes hotels, motels, condos, using someone else's home, or just camping under the stars. Don't look for any advice on camping here. While it can be quite enjoyable, it's not the kind of vacation most people like to take. Instead you will learn how to pay absolutely nothing, or pay just a small percentage of the going rates for a luxurious hotel or its equivalent.

## Meals

While we each have our daily calorie requirements, there will be very few money saving ideas in this book for saving money on meals. Be sure you read the section on condos in Chapter 5. In general, if you try to avoid places where business people entertain, you will have avoided most of the higher priced restaurants. If you're on a tight budget, you can always take advantage of early-bird specials at many restaurants, or go to a local fast food establishment, or bring fried chicken back to your hotel room. However, if you follow the other advice in this book, you should be able to save enough money so you can actually afford to go to a nice Four Star restaurant. You should also have enough left over for a bottle of the best wine on the menu!

## Spending Money

Everyone is concerned with money today, and taking the annual vacation can put a significant drain on your bank account. Having an adequate amount of spending money in your wallet is absolutely essential. There are many things you can do to stretch your spending money on your vacation.

If cash will still be a problem after you have saved on your plane ticket and hotels, then you should seek counsel from a travel agency. Explain that you are looking for a place where the dollar will go far. Mexico, Portugal, Spain and most of the countries behind the Iron Curtain are good travel bargains because of the relative value of the American dollar in those countries.

There are a number of travel guides available in your library and at leading bookstores (example: Frommer's "Hawaii On $35 A Day" published by Simon and Schuster) which you should study before you travel. Most popular vacation destinations are covered by these books. They contain hundreds of ideas on money saving places to visit (often for free), reasonably priced places in which to stay, and restaurants which cost well below the average.

Also, several months before you take your trip, check with your travel agent and write to the Tourist or Visitor's Information Center at your destination. Ask for descriptive literature and be certain to ask if there are any discount coupons or booklets available. They often give you coupons which offer two meals for the price of one, discounts for major attractions, or dollars-off coupons for car rentals, film developing etc.

It is not always necessary to rent a car when you travel. You will find that public transportation is quite dependable and reasonable in most major cities. The Metro in Washington, D.C., for example, is relatively new and is quite cheap during non-peak hours. It will take you within a few blocks of just about anywhere you might want to go. Using public transportation also relieves you of the worry of driving in a strange city or country. You won't have to worry about parking your car every few hours and risking unnecessary parking violations either.

## Types of Vacations

There are probably as many purposes of vacations as there are vacationers. You might want to simply rest and relax, to visit friends or relatives, or to explore new places. Regardless of the purpose, vacations generally fall into one of three major categories.

First, there are organized package tours. These are sometimes called escorted tours. There are many different types, going to thousands of different places throughout the world. Most of these are motorcoach (bus) tours. There are tours for people with special interests such as wine-tasting, skiing, scuba diving, visiting historical points of interest, and hundreds of others. There are tours for people who want to spend a lot of time in a limited area - like 7 days in the Washington, D.C. area, and there are tours which cover 15 European countries in 13 days.

Some escorted tours include all transportation, meals, and hotels, with arrangements made for every stop. Others permit you some time to wander off by yourself for part of the trip. If you take an escorted tour, there is usually not much opportunity to explore on your own. It is almost impossible to create your own schedule. Times are arranged for morning departure, and appropriate stops are made for purchasing souvenirs, lunch and dinner. Some don't even let you choose your meal. This can be somewhat frustrating for individuals who like to sleep late occasionally, or who might like to sample another kind of food during the course of a trip. You will have to leave your suitcase in your room each morning, or bring it down to the lobby yourself. You will also generally sit in an assigned seat on the bus. In essence, you have to follow the scenario written by the tour operator.

Millions of people prefer the escorted tour, which is generally free of decision making. They can be very relaxing since someone else does the driving and the planning. Essentially, arrangements for your every moment are prearranged by a travel agent. If you have not taken the time to plan or read about your destination, and want to let someone experienced in the area show you the local points of interest, this might be the type of trip for you. Tours can be particularly attractive for people who don't like the idea of driving in a strange city or country.

Other tour packages offer more flexibility by providing you with only air and hotel. These packages usually have fixed dates, and seldom include sight-seeing. They often include a rental car, so you will be free to wander at your own leisure.

For many people, package tours are great money values. The people who put the package together (called tour wholesalers) have the advantage of receiving huge discounts from each travel supplier. If you were to make your own identical arrangements for air transportation, hotels, sight-seeing and meals, it would cost substantially more. If you had to pay "retail" for each piece, you could easily pay double for the same trip.

There are only a limited number of ways in which you can save money on tour packages. It is generally impossible to arrange for your own airline transportation, since this is usually part of the package price. You can often choose between economy, moderate or luxury priced hotels along the way. Normally you will not be able to select your own hotels and obtain discounts on a tour using the tactics described in these pages. However, be sure you read Chapter 14.

Be sure that you do not purchase a complete package tour unless everything included in that package meets your needs. As you read on, you will learn there are ways to pick and choose only the pieces of a vacation package which you want.

The second type of vacation will be referred to as the free-style vacation. Most vacationers choose this type. Before leaving on their trip, they obtain information about their destination and scrutinize the literature to determine what to do when they get there. They select their own airline and date and time of departure. They decide which hotel they will stay at. In essence they develop their own detail plans. This is what distinguishes an experienced traveler from a tourist.

Whether you make arrangements for airline, cruise, hotel, car rental, sight-seeing etc. on your own or through a travel agent, you will write your own scenario for your vacation. If you wish to spend 2 days in Rome, you can. If you want to play golf at 3 o'clock in the afternoon, you can. But if you happen to miss the native dance ceremony because you didn't know about it, you'll probably wish you had taken the organized tour instead!

Experienced travelers know that most of the very same sight-seeing tours, which other people have purchased as part of an organized tour, can be arranged through a travel agent. They can be arranged for in the hotel lobby where you are staying. If you're not sure, check with the concierge, the bellman or the front desk clerk when you check in.

The big advantage to a free-style vacation is the flexibility which it affords. It almost always saves you money as well, since you choose only those sight-seeing trips which are of interest to you. You make your own plans for meals, souvenir shopping etc., and you can schedule your own hours of activity.

It is this type of vacation which will enable you to achieve the greatest possible savings. You can choose your own airline from which, you will learn, you can obtain free or discounted tickets. You can choose your own hotel for which you might also obtain free or discounted stays. And you can choose your own rent-a-car firm which might allow you several free days usage.

There are also packages available through a travel agency which may include air, hotel and car rental. These also afford you the opportunity to travel at your own pace and to do what YOU want to do. If you have your free airline tickets and want to use them for your trip, ask your travel agent about purchasing a "land package." These include only the hotel and car rental.

The third type of vacation is also a free-style vacation - the only difference being that little, if any, planning will go into the trip. This will result in your spending a lot more money than you should. Failure to plan well in advance will mean that you will pay the highest prices for your airline tickets and hotel. You will probably miss out on a lot the destination has to offer, and you will probably have little to reflect on when you return home.

Planning, not only to save money on your travel arrangements, but also to get the most out of your destination, is essential to becoming a "professional" traveler. With this book you will come to understand the secrets of cost effective travel. You will no longer travel as a "tourist" or pay full price for your vacation.

# 2

# TRANSPORTATION

The most common vacation in the United States is driving the family car to a destination. Convenience and economy are the obvious reasons for this choice. Many people are quite content to go to nearby locations year after year, whether it be the mountains or seashore. Often this is the only way they can bring the children and the dog with them. More often, they are concerned with the rising costs of vacations using public transportation. And they are quite justified.

The second most popular vacation is to go by plane. With over 475 million airline tickets being sold in the U.S. last year, flying has almost become as routine as going to the grocery store.

Today there are more than 100 large scheduled airlines in the U.S. and Canada which serve almost every city with a population over 50,000. Nine of these - American, Continental, Delta, Eastern, Northwest, Pan Am, TWA, United and USAir account for more than 85% of all U.S. passengers.

There are also hundreds of additional regional airlines which fill in the gaps and serve smaller communities. More than 800 communities have air service available today. Each airline has a different style, and each has its own market to which it caters.

## Classes Of Airline Service

There are three classes of service offered by most airlines: First, Business and Coach. You should understand the differences between each since you will soon have to decide which type of free or reduced price ticket you would like. One thing you should not forget is that regardless of the class of service, the plane will arrive at the same time, the flight will be just as bumpy, and you will probably see the same movie if there is one. Apart from these things, the main differences will be the comfort and level of service you will receive and the price you will pay.

## First Class

First Class is always located in the front section of the plane, and is usually restricted to the first 3 to 6 rows. Some people feel the ride in the front is somewhat smoother. Actually the difference in ride is negligible, but it is generally quieter since the plane's engines are always "aft" of this section. Seating in First Class is always more comfortable than else-where in the plane. Seats are 5 to 6 inches wider, and there is much more leg room (usually 7 or 8 inches more). In fact the width of 2 first class seats is about equal to 3 coach seats in the back of the plane. On overseas flights, there are often leg rests which can be pulled out for additional comfort.

Perhaps the nicest thing about first class is the additional service afforded. There are more flight attendants per pas-senger than in other sections of the plane. Flight attendants with the highest seniority usually receive these assignments. All flight attendants are quite knowledgeable about the aircraft and the airline. Because of their heavy travelling experience, attendants in the first class section are usually better informed about your destination than attendants in other sections of the plane. Once their tasks have been completed on a long distance flight, these attendants will often take the time to chat about your destination, recommend a good restaurant etc. You shouldn't choose First class service for this feature alone.

Another nice feature of flying First class is the food and beverage service. Your First class meal might very well be prepared fresh aboard the aircraft. You generally receive an appetizer, cloth napkins, free wine with your meal, and often even an ice cream sundae. These types of amenities are never seen in the back of the plane. Alcoholic beverages which sell for about $3 per bottle in Coach are dispensed free and freely. If you are so inclined, you can actually imbibe nonstop from coast to coast!

Movies, when available, are free, and upon your arrival, you often receive a copy of that day's newspaper to read while you sip on a glass of champagne! First class service is great for those who can afford it. It is especially nice when you are taking a long cross country trip or across an ocean. If you are taking a "special" trip for your honeymoon or that once-in-a-lifetime vacation, you might want to consider treating yourself to this luxury.

Fares for first class can be as much as twice the cost of a Coach ticket. Generally, airlines do not offer many discounts for these seats. As with all airline tickets, if you follow the advice in this book, these can be purchased for up to half of the normal full cost. And just because you see the First class section filled up each time you walk through a plane, don't think that all these people have actually paid for this service. When an airline knows that all of its First class seats have not been purchased, they will almost always "upgrade" their most frequent passengers to these seats at no extra charge! Under the right circumstances, you can also be upgraded. Read on!

## Business Class

Business Class is offered by most of the major airlines, especially on longer flights. It is located between the First class compartment and Coach. Prices and level of service are

also in between the other two classes. Seats are more comfortable than coach, food service is similar to First class, and
the cost is often closer to First than it is to Coach. This is the
section people take when they would really like First class
service but just can't afford to pay top dollar.

## Coach Class/Economy

Coach seats represent 80-90% of all the seats on most planes.
These are the airline's bread and butter. Prices for these
seats can vary from full fare to heavily discounted. Service is
usually meager by most standards. Meals, when served, are
almost on a take-it-or-leave-it basis. Most carriers now offer
meals only when the flight is for more than two hours.
Alcoholic beverages are available for about $3 per bottle, $2
for wine, but canned soda is free. If there is a movie available,
you will have to pay from $3-5 for a headset. Storage for
your carry-on materials or overcoat is limited. In Coach
class, there may be as many as 5 people competing for the
same amount of storage space as only 2 people have to share
in the First class section.

Seating can be uncomfortable, and it is not uncommon to
have 3 seats close together, each only 16 to 18 inches wide.
Leg space between seats is restricted. If you are above
average in height your knees may have a tight squeeze.
Needless to say, there is not much room to move about. This
can often lead to an uncomfortable trip, particularly when
your flight is more than 2 hours long.

What you have to remember is that these seats are much
more economical than seats in the First or Business class
sections. You will soon learn that there are ways to purchase
discounted tickets for First class which cost less than a full
fare (non-discounted) Coach ticket.

## Airline Deregulation

In 1978 the Federal government, under President Jimmy
Carter, decided to deregulate the airlines and let the
American free enterprise system take over. Prior to this, each
airline had to apply to the government for its rates to be
approved in advance, and had to serve certain cities (some

of which were not very profitable). They had to deal with bureaucratic red tape and delays. Congress felt that airline pricing and service would improve because of competition. As a result of deregulation, airfares are now often lower than they were ten years ago despite rising costs. For the average American, this was one of the best things that could happen. The level of service has, sadly, not improved much during this period. Competition continues to be extremely sharp and prices have dropped dramatically, putting the price of a plane ticket within the reach of the average person.

## Airline Rate Wars

Today each airline sets its own rates based on flight frequency and air mileage. Very often, rates reflect a competitive price which is determined by the market place. There is a fierce war being waged among the airlines to entice people to fly with them rather than with one of their competitors. It is very important for an airline to fill up each plane. No airline has an unlimited number of planes, so if a flight is not filled up, they cannot bring in a smaller plane. Airlines are exceptionally sensitive to prices and rates may change from day to day. When one airline announces a new rate, within days other airlines flying the same routes announce the same rate, sometimes going even lower.

Trying to keep track of who flies where, and what rates are in effect on any given day, has gone beyond human capacity. Today there are several computer networks to do the job. These are sponsored by the major airlines and allow them to update their fares almost immediately. Most travel agents use one or more of these computer systems to help them sort things out.

## Airlines Come and Airlines Go

During the last 10 years, many airlines have come into existence, several have gone out of business (remember Freddie Laker?), and some have merged into larger airlines (remember People's and Frontier?) Many smaller "regional" airlines have appeared to fill the gaps, servicing smaller cities which the larger airlines have avoided. There are now about 175 regional airlines throughout the country and this number is constantly changing. Some airlines like Braniff have even gone out of business and been resurrected. Sales of airlines are becoming a common occurrence. Donald Trump recently purchased the Eastern Airlines Shuttle (servicing Boston, New York and Washington D.C.) for his empire.

In early 1989, Piedmont and USAir merged into one company. The industry is now settling down, with no major takeovers or sales pending. This does not mean there will not be other changes in the future. The airlines are constantly shifting their strategies, servicing new cities and taking over control of regional carriers. You will soon learn that you should try to keep up to date on these changes.

# 3

# UNDERSTANDING AIRFARES

The largest airlines in the United States operate about 17 MILLION flights each year. There are probably 15-20 different fare types on each of these flights. Finding the best rate will probably be the greatest problem you will have to face in the world of travel, unless, of course, money is no object. Chances are that no one sitting within 10 feet of you on a plane will have paid the same price for their seat as you did. You must be certain that *you* are paying the absolute lowest fare available.

## Airline Philosophy

To understand airline fares, you first have to understand something about airline philosophy. Airlines, like any other enterprise, are in business to make money. Each flight is supposed to earn a profit. Besides the costs of the plane you board, the salaries of the pilots, flight attendants, baggage handlers and ticket agents who serve you, and the cost of the snacks or meals you receive, they must also cover the cost of their reservation centers, computers, management, advertising and, of course, the cost of the free tickets they give away. As mentioned earlier, competition has a way of forcing the fares down. Whether an airline likes it or not, and whether they make a profit or not, they find themselves in a position where they have to match the rates offered by their competitors.

## Airline Management

Airlines manage their business on a day to day basis paying attention to what is called "yield management." They pay particular attention to the "load factor" for each individual flight. The load factor is a percentage which compares the number of paying passengers to the number of seats available on a flight. A load factor of 60 means that a flight is 60% full.

It may surprise you to know that, although your last flight was probably packed full, the average load factor for all airlines is only about 60%. Smaller airlines have a lower factor, so your chances of finding an available seat are better on them. In 1987, not one U.S. airline had a load factor as high as 70% overall. It is because of this low number that the airlines are willing to reduce their rates to you.

When the load factor of a given flight is particularly low, the airline will take steps to increase it. One way is to increase the number of seats available at discounted fares. On the other hand, when the load factor is exceptionally high, they may reduce the number of cheaper seats and try to sell only the higher fares. In this manner they manipulate fares and try to steer discount customers to less crowded flights in order to balance out their individual flights. The flights you will be directed to are often for less desirable departure days or times of the day.

On many airlines, rate changes take place right up until the time of departure. If an airline were to offer all tickets on a particular flight at reduced fares, they might not be in business very long. Only a limited number of seats on any flight are made available at bargain fares. An airline might decide a month ahead of time that 5% of the seats on a New York to Los Angeles flight will be sold at $99 - the hyped-up advertised rate. Two weeks before the flight, if the load factor is not as high as expected, they might increase this to 10% of all seats; one week later 20% of the seats might be discounted.

## Rate Restrictions

If you look carefully at airline advertising, you will see comments in fine print like "not available on all flights," "only available from noon Monday through noon Thursday," or "limited availability." Advertised rates are generally very limited in number and have many restrictions attached. These may include a requirement to purchase your ticket 30 days or more in advance or penalties for cancelling your plans. Airlines seldom, if ever, advertise their standard or full fare prices. These are substantially higher, often more than double or triple the cost of the advertised fares.

## Severe Restrictions

Another tactic used by the airlines is to severely restrict all tickets (not just discount tickets) during heavy travel periods like Christmas, Easter and Thanksgiving. Often, they will manage these flights more closely than at other times of the year. For example, flights to the Caribbean at Christmas time, or to the Super Bowl city in January are seldom discounted. In fact, if it were possible, travel agencies and tour companies would purchase these tickets in bulk and later resell them for a hefty profit.

To prevent this from happening, airlines often reserve these flights many months in advance, even up to a year before the flight's date. What they do is to make the flight appear to be full on their computer. When a reservationist or travel agent inquires about it, the flight appears to have no space available. In reality, there might be very few seats sold for that flight.

The airline will eventually take reservations on a "waitlist" basis only, and then close the waitlist at a certain time. While this may seem unfair, the airlines do this because a very high number of people make reservations on a speculative basis and then "no-show." This leaves the airline with too many empty seats. Several months before the departure date, the airline carefully confirms each waitlisted customer, and generally requires that the tickets be paid for within a short period of time. Thus it makes certain that only sincere travelers are included.

You should be aware of this if you are planning to go to a very popular destination at a popular time. It is also not very likely that you will be able to obtain a discount. If you really have to travel at that time, you should reserve as much as a year ahead of time. If you are not successful at first, then you should keep on trying on a daily basis. You must learn NOT to take "not available" for an answer. Don't forget to ask if you can be waitlisted. You might just get lucky.

# 4

# SHOPPING FOR THE BEST AIRFARE

Before you start this section, try this experiment: Choose a city which is a long distance away from your home - at least 1000 miles away. Call each of two different airlines at least twice on the same day. Also call two different travel agencies on the same day. Tell each that you want to know the best fare available for one person travelling one week from today. Tell them that you will be staying for a total of ten days and returning back home. Write down the different fares you are quoted.

If you are like most people, you will probably find that you will receive at least 4 different "best" fares out of the 6 calls you made. You will probably also find that there are huge differences between the highest and the lowest fares quoted. If you are serious about saving money on your travel, it is essential that you understand the nature of airline fares.

Full fare or "standard" tickets for Coach, Business, or First class are the highest (worst) fares which you will have to buy. You will usually pay full fare 1) if you don't try to find another lower fare well before you travel, or 2) if you go to the airport at the last minute without a ticket. There are a host of discounted and promotional fares which are also available, if you know how to find them. These are sometimes called Supersavers, Maxsavers, Eurosavers, APEX and many others without any catchy name.

Each of these fares has a separate set of rules which might not always be made known to you unless the rules are severe. Such rules might involve whether you can change the dates or time of day you want to travel. Some restrict whether any of your money will be refunded if you can't travel, or whether you can switch to another airline if your plans change. They often require a minimum or maximum number of days away which might be too much or too little for your plans. Furthermore, some fares are only available if you purchase your tickets 30 days before the flight, some are 14 days, and others only 3 days before.  Each airline has its own restrictions, and to complicate matters, sometimes they even make exceptions to these rules, adding more restrictions or easing them.

As a general rule, the higher the price of a ticket, the fewer restrictions there will be. Since you will be seeking lower fares, be warned - the lower the price you pay, the more complex the restrictions will become. If there is any likelihood that your travel plans will change, be especially mindful of these restrictions.

The difference between the lowest discount fare and the standard fare for a plane ticket might be as much as $500 for any given flight. Knowing what to ask for, where to look and using every possible trick can result in tremendous savings in the price you pay. The keys to obtaining the lowest possible fare are planning, flexibility and persistence.

## Planning Your Attack

Long before you decide exactly where and when you want to take your vacation, you should be watching for airline promotions on TV and radio as well as in the newspapers. Other opportunities including "package deals" which include hotel etc. may be offered by travel agencies, hotels or tour operators. Get a rough idea as to how much a vacation might cost from this research.

Plan your trip as much in advance as possible. Wise vacationers usually have their plans made at least nine months ahead of time. This is really important since you will be able to take full advantage of fares which require advance purchase.

Plan your trip based upon your available time. If possible, try to plan your flights, both to your destination and returning home, for what the airlines consider "off-peak" periods. *This cannot be stressed enough.* If you can allow for some flexibility in your travel plans, you can save up to 50% on your ticket price!

Off-peak hours are usually from 11 p.m. until 5 a.m. You may have heard about "red-eye" special rates from the West coast to the East which leave at about 11 p.m. This might not be your first choice, but tickets on these flights are much cheaper than on the 9 a.m. flight to the same city.

The airlines operate at nearly full capacity from noon on Thursdays, throughout the weekend, and on into Monday until about noon. It is during these peak periods that most business people travel. Most vacationers who pay full fare also travel during this period. From noon Saturday until noon Sunday are sometimes considered off-peak since fewer people travel during this 24 hour period.

During peak periods, the airlines can charge just about anything they want and get it! People are always willing to pay the price when they have only limited control over their travel plans or when they have not properly planned their trip.

You will also find that special promotional rates are much harder to find during peak periods. This occurs because thousands of people may be trying to find them, and also because the airlines may designate only a small portion of their available seats for these fares. Later on in mid week, the same flight may have many more seats available at these discount rates. The airlines refer to this manipulation as "capacity control." Generally, the earlier you purchase your tickets, the better chance you have of obtaining a lower fare.

Therefore, if you do not plan well in advance and obtain the lower fares, you should give serious thought to altering your travel dates. If at all possible, arrange with your employer to take your vacation from Tuesday of one week through Tuesday of the following week. If your employer is flexible or if you are self employed or retired, you will have a much better opportunity to take advantage of discount fares. Then plan your departure for Monday evening or Tuesday morning when the lower fares are more readily available.

## Finding Out About Rates

You may deal with an airline either directly by using their toll free telephone number or by using a travel agent. As an educated traveler, you should use both! While a travel agent can be a great help in planning your trip, some recent surveys have shown that they do not always make a thorough effort to find the lowest available airfare.

Since it costs you nothing to call, get in touch with the airline directly. Be sure to call several airlines which fly to your chosen destination. Appendix A at the back of the book contains a list of these free telephone numbers. You can also obtain their toll free number by dialing 1-800-555-1212. Since these lines are usually quite busy, the best time to call is after normal business hours.

When you call, tell the reservation agent where you want to go and how many people will be travelling with you. One of the first questions the reservationist will ask is "When do you want to travel?" To get the absolute lowest fare, tell them that you have not yet decided when you want to fly. Explain that you are concerned with obtaining the lowest available fare. Or indicate approximately when you want to travel. Then you can alter your travel plans to fit the fare. A ticket for today's flight might cost you $400. It might be $350 if you are travelling in three days, and it might be as low as $200 if you are travelling two weeks from today.

Ask the airline for its flight schedule if you do not already have a copy of their timetable. Pick more than one flight which would be acceptable to you. Do not lock yourself in to saying that you only want to travel "at 9 a.m." Ask if they have any discount fares available for those flights. Ask about a special promotional fare by name if you are aware of any. You should know about these from newspapers, TV and radio advertisements. If they have no discounted fares for the time period you have chosen, ask about the availability of these fares at other times of the day. Most people like to travel in the early morning hours. Consider travelling on the prior evening or later on in the day. You will often find discount fares available on these flights.

If there is more than one major airport within a reasonable distance from your home, then ask about flights from those airports. If you live near Chicago, check on flights from Midway or Milwaukee. If you live near New York, check on MacArthur, Westchester and Newark airports. San Francisco residents should check on flights from Oakland as well. On the other hand, when you are going TO a destination, check on flights going to nearby cities, as above. This is where your flexibility comes in.

You should always ask if there are any other discount or promotional fares available or if there is any way you can save even more money. Don't hesitate to become too friendly with the person on the other end of the phone. They deal with more discourteous people than you would imagine and normally welcome a friendly conversation. Most airline reservation people will not volunteer discount information to you, but will be more than willing to help you if you ask!

Most airlines do not offer discounts to the general public. If you are a member of the military, be sure to ask if there are any special discounts available. USAir for example, will grant a 50% discount to active duty military personnel and their dependents, even if the dependents are travelling alone. You will have to show identification when you purchase your tickets, and again when you travel.

You should also consider changing the length of time you will be travelling. Some of the best discount fares require that you stay over at least one Saturday, or that you be away at least 7 days. If you are planning a shorter trip, try to find a good reason for staying an extra day or two. You should also be aware that, if you purchase one of these tickets and later decide to cut your trip short by a few days, the airline will very seldom honor your original fare. You will almost always end up paying an additional amount.

When you find the best fare, make your reservation. Be certain before you make your phone calls that you can commit everyone travelling with you to your schedule. Be sure to ask for and write down the confirmation number. It is also very important that you ask if there are any restrictions on the ticket. You should inquire about any cancellation penalties. Many tickets are non-refundable if you change your plans. Others may have a specific cancellation fee, particularly on overseas flights. Be sure you know how long you have to pay for or pick up your tickets. Most airlines require you to pay for your tickets at least 7 days (often more) before your trip. Ask whether you can change your flight plans and what the final date for changing plans will be.

Sometimes an airline will honor a quoted fare even if the fares are increased after you made your reservation. Usually they will honor the original fare after you have paid for your ticket. Be certain to ask if your fare is guaranteed, especially when you pay for your ticket 30 days or more in advance. You don't want any surprises when you arrive at the airport.

If you are unable to obtain a bargain fare, you have to be persistent. When you are told that a particular fare is not available, what they might really mean is that the fare is not available "at that moment." Call back a few hours later, and again a few days later. And keep calling every few days. You might have been unlucky on your first attempt or you might have spoken to a new employee. Hopefully, the next time you call, you will talk to another reservationist who might be more familiar with the computer system.

There are two other things which might occur in the mean-time: 1) people who received discounted fares might have changed plans and cancelled their reservations, making that fare available again, or 2) the airline might have "opened up" more seats at the fare you are requesting. This happens with some regularity. If the airline starts with 5% of its seats offered at a discount, and later determines that the flight has not been filling up to its expectations, they might increase the allocation to 10%. Sometimes this happens on Monday morning after management has had a chance to review how weekend sales went. More often, these decisions are made by computer and could occur just about any time. If you are trying to obtain a discounted fare which requires a 7 or 14 day advance reservation, be sure to call the airline several times on the day the deadline occurs. There are many cancellations at the last moment, and of course the airline could also have added more seats at the lower fare.

Even if you are able to find a great rate by dealing directly with the airline, be certain to visit your favorite travel agent. They are very familiar with the current situation in the travel industry. They might be aware of new airlines or charter flights going to your chosen destination. They might know of other special promotions going to your destination. They usually have one or more computer systems at their disposal, and may be able to improve on your rate or even offer you a cost saving package. If they are unable to help you find a better price, you should at least be able to pay for and receive your tickets through the travel agent. This is possible even when you made the reservation directly with the airlines yourself. Be sure to carefully read Chapter 13 which will show you how to select a travel agent.

# 5

# LODGING

When it comes to arranging a place to stay on your vacation, there are many more alternatives than there were for your airline tickets. Your choices range from exclusive luxury hotels to camp grounds. Many of the very best luxury hotels don't advertise so their clients can maintain their anonymity - at prices you would not believe. In between there are the luxury hotels, condominiums, timesharing, moderate hotels, economy hotels, motels, budget hotels, and a host of other alternatives.

Before you can begin to save on your lodging costs, you have to consider the various types of accommodations available and what to expect when you arrive.

## Types of Hotels

Hotels, like airlines, try to distinguish themselves from their competitors based on the level of service they provide. Prices are almost directly related to this. The term "service" has been somewhat stretched over the last ten years. It now includes not only the attention and courtesy provided by the staff, but also the furnishings, facilities and other amenities which are available.

## Service

Efficient and friendly service can be taught but costs a hotel quite a bit of time and money. Training of hotel personnel ranges from formal 2 or 3 week courses at a training center to on-the-job instructions which may last only a few hours. Service with a smile, whether it is the clerk at the front desk or the room service waiter, is largely a function of the individual's mood at the moment you deal with them. The advantage which "better" hotels have is that they generally pay their employees more and offer better benefits, which implies that they can hire the cream of the crop. But you will pay for this.

## Location

The biggest differences you will notice between the various classes of hotels will probably be the location and the decor. Being located right on the prime stretch of beach or on the main street in town has its benefits, but locale has its price. Whether the hotel owns the land or rents the space, you are going to pay for it.

When you travel to a popular destination, consider staying in hotels away from the main metropolitan area. You will often find that the savings can easily offset the additional cost of transportation back into the main city you are visiting. In addition to the monetary savings, you will find that the life-style is more relaxed and your stay can be much more enjoyable. The cost of meals will also be more reasonable in the suburbs.

## Facilities

Free pickup at the airport, spacious lobbies, deep pile carpeted floors, chandeliers in the lobby, a choice of fancy restaurants in the lobby area, roof top swimming pools and convention halls are great features which can be found in the better hotels. Whether you use and enjoy these facilities or not, and whether you are impressed with all the crystal and the comfort, you are going to pay for it.

Larger room size, more expensive furnishings, bigger bed size, remote control for your TV, shampoo in your bathroom and separate wash basins are great features which are not offered in every hotel. Again, whether you are impressed by these things or not, they will be reflected in your room rate.

At the lower end of the hotel spectrum are the economy or budget hotels which still provide the essential room for a night. Desk clerks may not be wearing fancy uniforms, but rather might be in their jeans. The lobby may be a 12 foot square room with cheap tile, but serves the purpose for checking in. The pool, if there is one, may be near the back parking lot, and will be significantly smaller. They will probably be located several blocks off the main street, and may even be a few highway exits away from the action. Towels and soap may be on the small size, and you may not even have a dresser in which to store your clothes. Since they have not invested as much money in their property and facilities, the rates they charge might be perhaps one fourth of the price you would pay for the luxury hotel.

In between the two extremes described, there are a whole range of hotels, motels, motor inns, and guest houses. Prices will range from incredibly high to suspiciously low.

## Identify Your Interests

Before you decide on a hotel, you have to consider what your interests are. Will you be spending much of your time at the hotel, or will you be sight-seeing all day and using your room only for a few hours rest? Do you like to eat your meals in the hotel or nearby, or do you like to explore the city and eat elsewhere? Do you like to socialize at a hotel bar or are you willing to travel a mile to go to the beach? Will you be taking your dog with you or can you get to the hotel from the airport without a car? The most important consideration will be how much you are willing to pay for a room. Once you answer some of these questions, you will probably have a feel for the type of accommodations you are looking for. Today, it is possible to find a room for anywhere between $20 to $150 a night in just about any medium sized city. Prices in major metropolitan areas range from $40 to $250. It is not necessary to stay at a top name chain of hotels to have a nice vacation. There truly is something for everyone.

## Know What to Expect

You can be reasonably certain of what to expect if you decide to stay at a hotel which is part of a major chain. A visit to the nearest Marriott or Motel 6 will give you a good idea of what to expect when you arrive at the other end. It's primarily the view from your window which changes from place to place within a chain of hotels. Try the restaurant at the local chain hotel. The atmosphere will be almost identical, and the menu will not be much different either, although prices will probably be higher wherever you are going. They always seem to be!

Directories published by the major chains may be requested free, and indicate the facilities available in a particular location. Most even have miniature road maps which will give you an indication of the hotel's distance from popular attractions.

Non-affiliated or independent hotels are another option. One problem is that you can never be certain of what to expect until you arrive. If this is the way you decide to go, try to obtain a brochure from the hotel or from your travel agent before you go. A recommendation from a friend or travel agent can be somewhat comforting before you see the place.

There are a number of other references which you can and should use before you select a non-chain hotel. Two of the most helpful are the AAA Tour Books (published by the American Automobile Association) and the Mobil Travel Guides. The Mobil Guides are available at most book stores and cover various regions of the country for about $8.95 each. The AAA books for each state or group of states are available free if you belong to one of more than 150 affiliated American Automobile Associations. Annual membership in AAA costs about $25-35 and includes a number of other worthwhile benefits. These include discounts at a number of hotels and a preferred rate from some of the major car rental companies.

Both travel guides offer excellent reviews of attractions for each area and sometimes offer discounts for these attractions. Your main purpose in reviewing these books however, should be to review their extensive list and descriptions of hotels. Most hotels listed in both guides are independent, non-chain hotels and are rated for your reference. Each guide has its own rating system. Mobil uses 1 to 5 stars while AAA uses 1 to 5 diamonds. Each hotel or motel is visited periodically and independently evaluated by these organizations. Each guide describes its rating system in the front of its books. For example, to receive two diamonds or stars, a hotel must have a color TV in every room among other things.

One mark generally means that the place is acceptable while five is outstanding. The greater the number of marks, the nicer a place will be - and the higher the prices will be. Price ranges for various types of rooms (single, double with one bed, etc.) are listed for each hotel, and are shown for each season of the year. Rates obviously go much higher when the area is "in season."

Sometimes the range of rates cited is quite wide; for example a double room might be $25-45 per night. Sometimes the rates listed are guaranteed to members of AAA, so it could be well worth joining that organization and be certain of what you will be paying each night. The descriptions in both guide books explain what you can expect to find - whether there is a swimming pool, laundry facilities, restaurant nearby, etc. These books can be very helpful in making your decision for a hotel.

## Obtain the Best Rate

Any hotel you decide upon may be reserved in one of three ways - through your travel agent, through their nationwide reservation center (for large chains), or by dealing directly with the hotel.

Your travel agent may be able to reserve you a room through their computerized reservation system. If you book through their system, you will receive one of the listed rates. These rates may not always be the best rates available. The systems used by travel agencies have only a limited number of hotels listed for each destination - usually the higher priced ones.

When you inquire about hotel accommodations, don't hesitate to ask your travel agent if they have looked in some of the handbooks and manuals which are available. These list almost all hotels in an area. Ask them to look at The Official Airline Guide (OAG) Travel Planner or The Hotel and Travel Index. Don't hesitate to ask to look at these books yourself. You might find a hotel which appeals to you.

Obviously, a travel agent can make a reservation for you for just about anyplace in the world. Just because the hotel is not on a computer system should not stop a travel agent from making a telephone call or writing a letter for you.

Finding all the chains of hotels and determining whether they have a property in the city you are going to visit can be a time consuming and frustrating exercise. If you have allowed enough time, call all of the major chains at their toll-free 800 telephone numbers and request a copy of their current directory. A list of the most popular chains can be found in Appendix B at the back of this book. Or you can call 1-800-555-1212 (no charge) and ask for the number for any other chain or individual hotel (providing they have toll free service).

If you are looking for lower to moderate priced accommodations, be sure to call Best Western, Comfort Inns, Days Inns, Econo Lodge, Friendship Inns, Holiday Inns, Howard Johnsons, La Quinta, Motel 6, Quality, Ramada, Red Roof, Rodeway, Super 8, and Travelodge. The most popular moderate to higher priced chains are Hilton, Hyatt, Inter-Continental, Marriott, Sheraton, Stouffer, Red Lion and Westin. These chains have properties located in most popular vacation destinations, and are very competitively priced.

Once you have their directory, you can determine if there is a hotel in the city where you are going. More importantly, you can find out their rates, what facilities they have available, which credit cards they accept, etc. Or you can call the toll-free number and discuss this information with the reservationist.

## Understand Hotel Rates

Hotels, particularly the bigger chains, price their rooms somewhat like the airlines price their seats. A certain number may be offered at a low promotional rate, and the number of rooms available at that price is subject to change. With this in mind, it is important that you try to reserve as much in advance of your trip as possible. Just as with the airlines, don't hesitate to call them back a few days later and ask about discounted rates. You just might be able to obtain a better rate.

One thing you should be aware of in respect to hotel pricing is that you will pay more for "location." In many hotels, rooms on the upper floors generally cost more than lower floors. These cut down on the amount of noise you might expect near the bar, restaurant and lobby. In resort areas, rooms near the swimming pool will cost more than those at the far end of the hotel. These afford you more convenience for which you must pay. In other hotels, rooms with a view of the ocean, bay or lake will cost more than one facing away from the nice scenery. Essentially, you may pay as much as 30% more for a quality location. Be sure to ask if there are rooms available in less desirable sections of the hotel.

When you are shopping for rates, ask about rates for the exact period you are planning to stay. Because of seasonal differences, there may be large variations in prices. A rate quoted for next week may be significantly higher (or lower) than on the nights you will be there. As in dealing with the airlines, inquire about any promotional offers you may have heard or read about. Be sure to ask if there are any ways you can save more money. Hotel rates are generally not as confusing as airline rates, and you will find fewer rates to choose from.

## Discounts At Hotels

Today, almost everyone checking into a hotel receives some sort of discount. You must make sure that you do not pay the full "rack" rate. Most hotels offer a "corporate" or a "commercial" rate, usually a few dollars lower than the rack or standard rate. Ask if they have one of these business rates, and if you are eligible for one. If you work for a large company like GE, IBM, Ford etc. specifically mention who you work for. They may offer you a discount anyway. It is also a good idea to check with the travel department where you work before you start. Determine if there are any corporate rate plans with any hotels before you start to make your calls. Sometimes you only have to show a business card to qualify for these discounts. At other hotels you only have to request a corporate rate to receive it.

Almost every organization you belong to will have a discount plan for its members with at least one hotel chain. Unions, government worker's and teacher's organizations, credit card organizations, members of the military, and banks and credit unions almost always receive a discount. Don't forget to look for discount offers if you have joined AAA. Today, almost everyone is eligible for some type of discount. If you belong to more than one group, compare your discount rates. For one you might receive a 5% discount, and for another 10% - obviously, you should select the one with the best offer.

If you are a senior citizen, ask the hotel if they offer any special discounts. If you belong to AARP (American Association of Retired Persons, 1909 K St. N.W., Washington, D.C. 20049) ask about member discounts. Incidentally, you don't have to be retired to join AARP as long as you are over 50 years old and pay a $5 per year membership fee. Even if you don't belong to AARP, some hotels will give you a discount, although it may not be as high.

A number of popular travel clubs offer substantial discounts at specified hotels. Several offer you the second night free, or seven nights for the price of six. Several clubs list thousands of hotels offering these discounts which amount to about 50% off.

If you own stock in any major hotel chains, be sure to read the shareholder newsletters or annual reports carefully. Some major chains offer their stockholders special rates as low as $30 per night provided the hotel is less than 80-90% full. Some announce these rates and others remain silent about them. If you are not certain, write to the Corporation's Secretary and ask if there are any special rates available. It might very well be worthwhile purchasing a few shares of stock in a company which offers such a discount, provided that you will be able to use their services often enough. Considering today's brokerage fees, you would need to stay quite often just to recover these fees.

## Call Hotels Directly

After you make a reservation through the central reservation number, call the hotel where you would like to stay directly. You can ask for this number from the reservationist, or, if you have the hotel directory, it is generally listed. There are many times when the central reservation office is not aware of special promotions being offered by each property. Although this call will generally not be toll-free, it could save you much more than the cost of the call. Ask to speak to the reservations department. It is not necessary to indicate that you already have a reservation. Go through the same line of questioning as you did with the central reservation office above. Be sure to ask about any special promotional rates which might be in effect. You might be surprised to learn that 10-15 percent of the time you will be able to improve on the rate you received.

Don't be disappointed if the reservation center advises that there are no rooms available for the nights you want. Although this might be true, many of the larger chains have a large number of franchise locations. These local owners have to pay a fee for every reservation received through the main number. They often put aside a number of rooms which they hope to be able to sell on their own without having to pay this fee. If you are told there are no rooms available, and this is the place where you really want to stay, pick up the phone and call the hotel directly. Chances are fairly good that you will be successful.

## Shop When You Arrive

There are a few things you can do when you arrive at your destination to save even more on your hotel rate. Most airports have a board or directory of hotels which is usually located near the baggage claim area. Call a few local hotels and ask about their rates. Of course, you are taking a chance on the quality of the hotel when you do this. And, of course, you should never rely on this practice alone. You should NEVER travel without having at least one reservation for a room. You just can't tell if there will be a convention in town when you arrive. You might find that there is not a single room to be had. Shop for rates, and then make a decision. If you have a reservation at another hotel, be certain to cancel it.

There is another technique which sometimes works in smaller towns, and is especially effective if you are driving. If you wait until after 6 p.m. before looking for a room, by then hotels will have a good idea of their available room status. When hotels have many extra rooms, they are more inclined to negotiate a rate. If you notice a lot of "Vacancy" signs or if the parking lot is not too crowded when you arrive, inquire about their rates. Offer the room clerk a few dollars less. Although some people find this difficult to do, you will find that, under these circumstances, you will often receive a discount. If you offer to pay cash, they will sometimes give you an even better rate than if you pay by credit card.

In addition, there are substantial savings to be had if you can arrange you vacation for an off-season time of year. Be sure you read Chapter 16 which covers this in more detail.

There are a few characteristics of individual hotel locations which can also help you save. Hotels which cater to business people are usually booked solid from Monday through Thursday nights. These same hotels are often quite empty Friday through Sunday nights and frequently offer large discounts for weekend stays. Most of these hotels are located near the main airport or in the heart of the downtown business district. Hotels and motels located along the highways between large cities have their heaviest business on weekends. They are anxious for business during the mid-week period. If you plan your travels well, you may be able to take advantage of these slack periods and save even more.

## Cancel Your Reservations

If you have a reservation at a hotel and change your plans, make sure you call them and cancel. It is just common courtesy. By doing so, you will be helping the hotel as well as other people who have waited until the last minute. More importantly, if you have guaranteed your reservation (see Chapter 11), be absolutely certain that you cancel. If you have given a credit card number, make sure you also receive a confirmation number or the name of the person you speak to when you cancel. This will help if the hotel later bills you for not showing up.

## Use Your Own Condo

That's right - Your own condo! You probably know some people who own condominiums in resort areas. They go there every year for their vacation, or even permit friends to stay there when it's not being used. A nice condo in a resort area can easily cost $100,000 and higher. Unfortunately it's quite a steep price to pay 1) when you don't have that kind of money or 2) when you cannot use it for more than a few weeks each year.

There is a way to be a condominium owner for only a fraction of the price. It comes with a number of advantages which full-time owners don't have. The concept is called timesharing. With timesharing, a developer doesn't sell ownership of an apartment to one individual. They sell one week portions in each condominium to each of 50 people. The extra week or two each year are normally reserved for redecorating. Once a year, each owner is required to pay a maintenance fee which generally ranges from $150-250. This fee is similar to the $300-600 monthly fee which a full-time owner might have to pay. The fee covers common costs like maintenance, taxes, furniture replacement, etc.

There are many different aspects to owning a timeshare, but the result is the same. Once you are an owner, the condo is yours to use for that specific week each year. Since you own it, you can use it - no extra charges are involved. This is a great way to save on hotel costs, especially if you like to go to the same place each year.

Using a timesharing condo has a number of advantages over staying in a hotel. First, you know exactly what to expect each time you stay there. Second, you can share the costs with other people; you can bring friends along. Rather than rent two hotel rooms on your trip, you will have your own place to stay in - with plenty of room. Third, timesharing condos are almost always decorated much nicer than hotels. They have full kitchens with complete sets of dinnerware. Dishwashers and washer-dryers are also usually included. You and your family can easily save a hundred or more dollars by preparing your own breakfasts, or by fixing a light lunch to take on your daily outings. If you like, you can prepare three meals each day, and save even more. But working in a kitchen can defeat the whole purpose of your vacation!

What if you would like to go somewhere else once in a while? With timesharing that is usually not a problem. If your timesharing is in a development which is affiliated with a large trading organization, you simply trade in your week and go somewhere else. These organizations permit you to trade your time for resorts all over the world for just a nominal handling fee. Your time can be exchanged for condos in Japan, Australia, Europe and hundreds of great vacation areas almost anywhere you can think of going.

With a reasonable effort, you should be able to find a timeshare condo available for sale in just about every state, in every resort area, and through resale agents. A week may cost anywhere from $1,000 up to $15,000 depending on when and where you decide to go. You must remember that once you own it, you may and should use it for your vacations every year. Be certain to inquire about the possibility of exchanging your property for resort areas where you would like to take your annual vacations.

## Take A Suite

There is a new trend today in hotels which you can use to save money if you are travelling with more than 3 or 4 people. Normally, if you stay at a hotel or motel, there will be a charge for each additional person, sometimes excluding children under a certain age. This can add a lot to your total bill. If there are 3 or more adults travelling in your party, there may be times when you will have to take two separate rooms.

A number of chains have recently opened "all-suite" properties. Each suite generally has a small kitchen and living area, and often have more than one bedroom. Some offer one bedroom with a fold-out sofa for additional people. Most times there are no charges for the extra people in your party.

Embassy Suites, Guest Quarters, Pickett, Comfort Inns, Quality Inns, Radisson and Residence Inns are among the larger chains which offer all-suite properties. Remember that these are not just suites within a regular hotel. All rooms in these locations are suites. The important thing to consider is that the cost for a suite is often less than the cost of two separate rooms at another hotel. You can even save a few dollars by preparing some of your meals in the kitchen provided.

There are other benefits to staying at an all-suite chain. All of them offer a free breakfast in the morning for you and all your party. Sometimes, it is nothing more than donuts and coffee. In other places, you have your choice of a full buffet style hot breakfast and you can eat all you want. Almost all offer a one hour cocktail hour in the evening which includes free drinks and snacks.

Now that we have discussed a number of alternatives for lodging on your vacation, let's find out how to get there.

# 6

# AIRLINE
# GIVEAWAYS

Beginning as early as 1981, the airlines began to compete for the business traveler with great enthusiasm by offering enticements to make him/her use their airline exclusively. The business traveler accounts for about 60% of an airline's customers, but buys about 80% of its tickets. You can imagine how important the business traveler is to the airlines.

To accomplish this, Frequent Flyer Programs were created. These programs track each customer's activity and how often he or she flies. Once travelers are enrolled in a program, they are enticed with offers of free tickets after a certain number of trips. Whenever possible a "player," as they are called, will do everything possible to travel only on that airline in order to "earn" free tickets faster. It was not long before every major airline in the United States and Canada was offering a similar program.

These programs were initially developed by the airlines to gain the loyalty of their business customers. While this has worked to a large degree, most business travelers now belong to more than one program. In this way, if they are forced to travel on another airline, they will still get something for nothing. These programs have become extremely popular with business travelers. So popular, in fact, that the airlines are now in a position where they are unable to end them. Pan Am tried to end its program abruptly in 1983 by requiring its players to redeem their mileage by June of 1984. During April and May, they found that most of their seats were occupied by free flyers. It was speculated that Pan Am lost in excess of a hundred million dollars in the second quarter of the year alone because of this mistake. The next airline to end its program will probably find all of its business customers switching to other airlines, because the other airlines will still have programs. So, fortunately, these programs will probably be here for a long time to come!

## Nothing Is Ever Simple!

The popularity of these programs within the business world has also gained the attention of governmental agencies. The IRS, as well as several of our Congressmen, would now like to tax the value of these free tickets. There are so many free tickets out there, Uncle Sam now would like a piece of the action! It will probably be a long time before this happens. The airlines would have a difficult time reporting this information to the government. And there are a number of legal questions to be answered first (free tickets are more like a discount, not additional income). The biggest legal problem centers around the business traveler who benefits personally from free trips when it was his/her employer who paid for the tickets.

Financial experts now want the airlines to record the value of their commitments for free trips on their books. The airlines are expected to fight this tooth and nail. It is estimated that airlines now owe almost $1 billion worth of free travel to their customers!

## The Airlines Go Silent

These programs have been extremely successful, not only for the airlines, but also for everyone who enrolls. If you haven't heard much about them, don't be surprised! The airlines don't often advertise that they are giving away free tickets. Perhaps you might have noticed that some airlines are not advertising as much on TV or in newspapers recently. This is because they can now reach their best customers directly through these programs.

If you have flown recently, you might have heard an announcement on your flight about these programs. Or you might have read something about it in the airline magazine. If you're like most people, however, you probably figured that it didn't pertain to you. You were mistaken! Anyone CAN and SHOULD join these programs. If you are serious about saving on your next vacation, you MUST participate in at least one of these programs.

If you are a business traveler, you probably already know something about these programs and may even belong to a few of them. But there is much more to be learned. If your business does not require that you travel, or even if you are not presently working, there are still plenty of opportunities to take advantage of them.

Each airline has created its program to be a little different from all the others. Generally, anyone can sign up to belong to a program. Most require that you be a US citizen or have a US mailing address. The three Canadian airline programs obviously were designed for Canadian citizens, but may be joined by anyone. Virtually all the airline programs cost nothing to join. You do not have to be a business person to belong to these programs. You don't even have to be employed.

## How To Find Out More

Simply call the airline, and request that frequent flyer information be sent to you. A complete listing of programs sponsored by U.S. and Canadian airlines is available in Appendix C. Many of the larger airlines will sign you up on the phone and give you a member number immediately. This is like opening a bank account with the airline. Once you have a number, it must be used each time you travel, whether you make a reservation yourself or through a travel agency.

## How The Programs Work

Once you join a program, you will be assigned an account number. Some airlines require that you place a sticker with this number on your ticket whenever you travel. Others track your travel activity by computer. A few require you to save copies of your tickets. Every time you fly, the airline will credit your account with "points." Usually, you will receive one point for each mile flown between two cities, regardless of how much (or how little) you pay for your ticket. The air distance between Atlanta and New York is 760 miles. Each time you fly this route you will receive 760 points or miles in your account.

Some programs give you one point for each trip you take; so a round trip would count for two points, one for each direction. Other programs give points based upon how much your ticket cost. A $78 round trip ticket would therefore earn you 78 points in this type of program. The most popular programs base their points on the actual air mileage you fly. This is important to remember. Whether you paid $99 for a Supersaver fare or $399 because you couldn't find a better fare, you will receive the same number of points in your account. Many programs also give you 1000's of points as a bonus just for joining up!

Most programs give you a minimum number of miles credit for each trip you take regardless of the distance of the flight. Therefore a 100 mile flight can count for as much as 1000 miles credit! This is a big advantage, especially if you take a number of short trips. A couple in Boston have taken two free First class trips to Hawaii over the last two years by taking advantage of this. They fly every second weekend to visit their son at college, which is less than 200 miles away. They each receive 2000 miles each weekend - 1000 for each direction. And to make things even better, they almost always find a special promotional rate of $39-59 for the trip.

Almost all of the airlines send you a statement once every month or two, reminding you of the points you have earned toward your free tickets. When you receive your statement, you should remember that the number of points you accumulate in your account has nothing to do with how far you can travel for free. 5,000 points does not mean that you get free travel for 5000 miles. Each program has its own rules, and these will be discussed below.

## What You Can Get

Each airline has a completely different chart of awards. Generally, the first award available is a free upgrade from Coach to a seat in First class. Those airlines which give you bonus points for joining usually give you enough points to get you half way to the first award level. The carrot is already dangling!

Other awards which most programs offer are: 50% off the cost of a Coach ticket, a free Coach ticket with a 50% discount for someone travelling with you, 2 free Coach tickets, 1 or 2 free First class tickets, and even large discounts toward cruises. Some programs offer other rewards like membership in their private airline clubs (luxurious lounges at the airports), and even an hour's use of a pilot's flight simulator (Canadian Airlines International). Obviously, the more points you earn, the greater your rewards. The choices are almost endless.

Most of the awards also come with additional bonuses - greatly discounted or even free hotels stays and/or car rentals. The Wardair program offers mini-vacations which even include your meals and beverages. These benefits should not be overlooked and will be covered in more detail later.

Some airlines require you to use the free tickets you earn for yourself. Others allow you to transfer them to members of your family. Some are not concerned with what you do with them as long as you do not sell them. And others don't even care if you sell them!

## What To Do Next

The first thing you should do after rereading this book is to drive out to the nearest airport and determine which airlines fly into your city. Every airline does not fly everywhere. Make a list of all the airlines which service your airport. Some of them may even have applications or literature about their frequent flyer programs at the ticket counter. You may even be able to sign you up when you stop there.

If you don't live near an airport, call some of the airlines which fly into the nearest airport (check your local Yellow Pages). Better yet, visit your travel agent, and ask for this information. If you don't live in a city which has major airline service, it will be well worth a drive to the nearest major city's airport for the same purpose. Many of the regional airlines serving smaller cities are affiliated with the programs of the major airlines. You may be able to earn credit by using these regional carriers as well.

Examine each airline's destinations on its departure board, and ask for a copy of their flight schedule. They may fly to some destinations which are not served directly from your city. When you get home, the fun begins! Carefully examine the flight schedules for each airline. Determine where you would most like to go on a vacation - hopefully where you will GO FOR FREE! Hawaii, Europe, the Caribbean, New York, Florida, California, or even a visit to Grandma can be yours. You decide where you would like to go. Read the airline's frequent flyer program literature carefully when you receive it. Then determine how many miles or points you will need to earn your award.

You will learn more about these programs before you should decide which one to join. It will be important to join one even if you have no plans to travel in the near future. As you will soon learn, *you don't even need to travel* in order to earn an award.

## Everyone Joins In!

With the success of the airline programs so widely recognized throughout the travel industry, it was not long before major hotels and car rental companies jumped on the bandwagon. First, they joined forces with the airlines.

When you receive your literature from each airline, it will include a list of their "travel partners." These hotel chains and car rental firms will give you points in your chosen airline program when you stay at their hotel or rent their car. Some programs only give you credit when you have travelled or will travel on their airline within a certain period of time, usually within 24 hours. Others will give you credit without this requirement. Thus, if you stay at a participating hotel, you could receive as many as 1000 points or miles in the *airline* frequent flyer program by identifying yourself as a member of that program. When you rent a car, you will also receive as many as 1000 points or miles for each rental. The American Airlines program once offered 10,000 bonus miles for purchasing a used car from their partner - Avis.

## Foreign Airlines

With the popularity of frequent flyer programs in the U.S. and Canada, many foreign carriers decided to sponsor their own programs. Many of them are also affiliated with domestic airline programs as you will see when you review Appendix C. If you have reason to travel outside North America on a frequent basis, you should certainly consider joining these programs as well. A complete list of foreign carriers sponsoring their own independent programs is included in Appendix D.

Foreign programs operate somewhat different from the domestic airline programs. Some of them only credit you for travel in First or Business class. Others will not consider you eligible until you have flown with them 3 or 4 times. Some of them offer free or discounted trips, while others offer only certain benefits such as upgrades, free use of luxurious lounges prior to your trip, advance seat selection etc. If you have occasion to travel overseas, be certain to contact the appropriate carrier for details about their program.

# 7

# HOTEL PROGRAMS

To make things even better, many hotel chains have created their own Frequent Guest or Frequent Stay programs. These are totally independent of the airline programs. Marriott began the trend in 1984; the latest to sponsor a program was Best Western in 1988. These programs operate much the same way as the airlines. You receive a certain number of points for each stay at one of their hotels. When you accumulate a certain number of points, you become eligible for free room nights or even longer vacations. The number of points you need varies depending on the program you join, but generally, they are similar.

Most of the big hotel chains are also affiliated with one of the airline programs. Since most of them have their own programs as well, a knowledgeable traveler can earn points in both programs for the very same stay! It is very common for a traveler to present a member number for the hotel's program, and a second member number for an affiliated airline program upon checking in. This is not only legitimate, but is encouraged by some programs. This practice is referred to as "double dipping." Now perhaps you can understand why it takes some people so long to check in to a hotel while you are waiting in line. Next time, hopefully, you will be able to take advantage of the same system!

Some hotels (like Marriott) will even give you a 25% bonus on *their* program if you fly in or out on one of their partner airlines. Just show your airline boarding pass - don't throw it away any more! They will also give you a 25% bonus if you rent a car from one of their car rental partners (just show them your rental contract), *and* they will give you credit in the airline program as well! These travel companies are anxious to give away points toward free trips just to have your business. A list of current hotel programs is contained in Appendix E at the back of this book.

### How Hotel Programs Work

Hotel programs also vary widely, and are more difficult to compare. Some give one point credit for every dollar spent (even for laundry and telephone calls). Some give one point for every ten dollars spent (only counting room rates, not including taxes etc.) Others give a fixed number of points for each night spent at the hotel.

Awards generally range from a 25 or 50% discount off a weekend stay, a free weekend stay, to a free week at a resort. The ultimate award is usually two free round trip airline tickets, AND a free week at a resort AND a free week's car rental. Other programs offer U.S. Savings bonds, clothing and electronics for the points you accumulate. The Holiday Inns Priority program, for example, offers televisions, freezers and furniture among its rewards.

Many programs are offered by hotels which cater to the business person who is usually on an expense account. Thus, their rates are generally on the high side. If you like to stay at better hotels or if you have an opportunity to travel on business and your company has a liberal policy on hotels, you should take advantage of the opportunity to earn additional points in these programs.

Hotel programs have different rules as to which room rates may be eligible for points. Some of them will give you points even if you stay at bargain rates such as weekend "specials" or "off-peak" reduced rates. Others will only give you credit for their full priced rooms.

Call or visit a number of the hotels which sponsor their own programs. Evaluate their programs the same way you did the airline programs. Examine the award schedule for each hotel which interests you. Consider the rates for each hotel - luxury, moderate or economy, and consider your own tastes in hotel style. Try to sort out the various programs and plan which program or programs you would like to join. This will be covered in more detail later.

## Additional Hotel Savings

When you are shopping for a hotel for your vacation (see Chapter 5), you should consider hotels sponsoring these programs. You may want to patronize them if you belong to their program. Also check with hotels which are partners in the airline programs you have joined.

Check through all your frequent flyer and frequent guest literature to see if there any special discounts at any of the chains you are considering. Hotels very often give discounts to members of their programs or airline programs with which they are affiliated. If you belong to a hotel's frequent guest program, ask if there are special rates available, even if discounts are not mentioned in the literature. Ask the hotel if there are any special rates for members of any of the airline frequent flyer programs. If you have joined any of them, give your membership number to obtain the discount. If you decide to stay at a hotel which offers a discount to an airline program member, and you don't already belong to that program, call that airline and join their program. Then call the hotel back with your new membership number and obtain the discount.

When you claim an award through an airline program, you will usually receive a hotel award as well. The awards you can expect will range from a 25% discount on a weekend visit to a free week at a resort hotel location. With higher level awards, you will have no problem saving money because your room will be provided with very little, if any, cost to you. Some hotels will require you to pay the sales tax on the free award; others will not even charge this nominal amount.

For awards at the lower end of the awards category, you will have to carefully evaluate the final cost you will have to pay. You will probably notice that the hotels affiliated with airline programs are usually higher priced chains. 25% off a weekend stay at a Sheraton means you still have to pay 75%. When you investigate the cost for one night, you might find that you will pay more there than the full cost of a room at a Holiday Inn or Quality Inn down the street. In fact, the airline programs don't really expect most people to redeem these lower level hotel awards.

When you call the hotel reservation center, make certain you indicate that you are planning to use an award certificate or a coupon for free or discounted nights. Many times, the hotels will "black out" popular holiday periods, or will restrict the number of people who can use a certificate at any time. If you are planning to stay additional nights after your award expires, make sure you know exactly how much it will cost.

# 8

# CAR RENTAL COMPANIES

After several attempts to sponsor their own independent programs, most of the car rental companies have decided to only participate in airline and hotel programs. Hertz, for example, participates in over 15 airline and hotel programs. You can take your choice of earning points in one program each time you rent a car.

National Car Rental sponsors its own independent program called The Emerald Club. For a membership fee, they will track your rentals and credit you with points (one per dollar spent). It offers awards ranging from three free weekend days of a car rental, to a one week vacation to Hawaii or Ireland. Their top award is the free use of a car for a year. This program is in addition to their participation in a number of airline and hotel programs. Call National at 800-962-7070 for further information.

Most of the other car rental companies (Alamo, Budget, Thrifty etc.) also participate in at least one airline or hotel program. See Appendix C and E and make certain that you review the list of car rental partners. Then whenever you rent a car, consider these companies.

As you have already learned, it is very important to shop for the best airline and hotel prices. It is no different when it comes to renting a car for your trip. Most of these companies have toll-free telephone numbers available. See Appendix H for a list of the major firms.

Car rental firms are generally not as sophisticated as airlines and hotels when if comes to managing their rates. They are very competitive, and frequently change prices. They seldom limit the number of rentals which are available at promotional rates. They often issue coupons or certificates through mailings, and often place coupons in their magazine and newspaper ads. Once you join the airline and hotel programs, you will be inundated with discounts and many special offers from each program's car rental partners. Many of these coupons have restrictions as to which dates the promotion is available, and they usually "black out" holiday periods. Be certain to keep these coupons until you need them for your vacation.

When you call to check prices, be sure to ask if there are any promotional rates in effect. You must be very specific when you inquire about rental car rates. A quoted rate may only be honored if you keep the car a minimum number of days. Bringing it back early can cost you much more per day. If you intend to return the car to a location other than where you rent it, be absolutely certain to mention this. There are very large drop-off fees involved when you do this.

Most car rental companies cater to the business traveler and offer very large discounts to almost every large and medium sized company. Be sure to check with your employer to see if they receive a discount from any car companies. If you belong to any professional or fraternal organizations, find out about their car rental discounts. You can even receive a discount when you subscribe to certain magazines. Don't forget about the discount you may be entitled to as a member of a travel club, AAA or AARP. And, of course, you will generally receive a nice discount simply because you belong to an airline or hotel program. When you inquire of the reservation agent, you may find that you have several discounts available. Make certain that you use the best one. If you are fortunate, you may find the best rate with the car rental company partner of your favorite airline or hotel program.

Most of the larger car rental companies locate their rental counters on the airport, usually near the baggage claim area. To operate in this location, they must pay a heavy fee to the airport authorities. These fees are passed on to you in their rental rates. There are also a number of smaller car rental companies which do not operate on the airport itself, but which offer a pickup service. They will drive you from the airport to their rental lot a few miles away. Their rates are almost always lower because they do not pay these concession fees to the airport. A number of off-airport companies will charge you an additional amount when there are airport fees involved. You should not overlook these firms because you can save a good deal of money on your rental. You should also consider the extra time involved in waiting for their bus and be certain to allow extra time when returning the car at the end of your trip.

# 9

# CHOOSING A PROGRAM

Perhaps you are thinking there are too many programs available and you're not sure which way to go. Think of the bright side... all of these companies are trying - very hard - to give away free trips! You only have to choose among them. Business travelers have the same problems, so most join four or five airline programs as well as two or three hotel programs. The more programs you join, the more literature you will receive, announcing each program's current bargains.

There will be times when you will be tempted to travel or stay somewhere just to take advantage of the bargains they offer - even if you don't have an otherwise good reason to travel. Actually, some of the bargains from hotels are irresistible and can help you earn points toward your free award. A number of people stay at these hotels just for a Saturday night to take advantage of special offers. It's also a good excuse to get away for a while! Over a few weekends, you can even earn free airline tickets. As an example, Inter-Continental Hotels recently ran a promotion where, if you stayed at certain hotels for only six nights, you could earn a free round trip Coach ticket. You could choose your free ticket from among four different airlines. This ticket was valid for travel anywhere in the Continental U.S. For staying only one additional night, you could receive an airline ticket to Hawaii, Mexico or the Caribbean. And for only two more nights (a total of nine), Europe could be yours for free. The cost of staying nine nights in the hotel (over a few weekends) would not have been much more than the full fare cost of the airline ticket alone. If you consider each weekend stay as a mini vacation, this type of offer could make earning your points truly enjoyable.

## Which Program To Join

At times, it can be difficult to sort through the benefits available to you. Unless you have frequent opportunities to fly or stay at hotels, (for example, if you occasionally travel for your company, or if you often visit someone in another city), you should *choose just one airline or hotel program and stick with it!* The entire process will be very simple if you concentrate your entire effort on just one program to achieve your goal.

## Other Reasons To Select A Program

There are many other benefits to belonging to a particular program which you should consider. Most airline programs have a number of hotel and car rental partners. Many of these partners also want your business when you travel - even if you don't travel on their airline partner. They offer special discounted rates to members of these programs. The daily rate for a car rental for someone walking in off the street might be about $45. It's not uncommon to receive a rate of $35-39 per day just because you belong to a frequent flyer program. A $5-10 savings per day adds up, particularly when you are renting a car for a week or more. Hotel partners frequently offer similar savings.

When you review the programs in Appendix C and E, be sure you also look at the list of travel partners affiliated with each program. If you see a hotel chain or car rental company which you really like to use, be certain to consider that program just for the added benefits. When you stay at a chain hotel or rent from a large car rental company, be certain to ask if there are any special rates for members of the programs you belong to.

You will never know about all the opportunities available for accumulating points unless you read each program's literature carefully. The United program, for example, offers 1000 points for each night you spend on a Holland America cruise. If you are planning such a vacation, be certain to join their program. A seven day cruise will earn you 7000 points.

## The Selection Process

After visiting the local airport and reviewing the airlines' schedules to determine where you want to go on your free trip, select the one airline program which best suits *your* needs. The most important thing to consider is whether the airline you choose flies to the place you want to take your free vacation. If you want to go to Europe, don't pick an airline which doesn't fly there unless it has other airline travel partners which do. Make certain that you also give serious consideration to the hotel programs. Call them to determine if they have a hotel in a city which you would like to visit. Select the one hotel program which seems most promising to *you*. Then narrow your choice down to ONE of these two programs based on your own life-style. Select the one which will give you the best opportunity to earn your free vacation.

In choosing your program, the thing you should be thinking about most should be how easy it will be to achieve your goal. You will want to consider the bonuses you will receive for joining, and any flights or hotel stays you might be taking in the future for which you would receive credit.

You will want to consider if the program has a time limit on it, and whether you can earn the required number of points in that time. Several airline programs have limited the amount of time in which you can accumulate credit. Alaska, American and United allow you only one year. Pan Am has a two year period. After the programs expire, you have to start over again. At the present time, there are no time limits on any other airline programs but this is always subject to change. Considering your individual spending patterns, you should probably avoid these programs unless you think you can reach your desired goal in the required time frame.

You will also want to evaluate alternative ways of receiving credit, especially by using an affinity credit card. This will be discussed in Chapter 11 in much more detail. Remember that you will be rereading this section again and you will understand the importance of these cards your second time through.

After evaluating all these things, join the program in which you will feel most comfortable, and you will be on your way toward your first award. This program will be referred to as "your" program, the program of your choice.

There is no cost to join most of these programs. Holiday Inns, Sheraton, Lan Chile and National Car Rental charge modest enrollment fees. Since most airlines and hotels provide toll free telephone numbers, join several programs which appeal to you. In this way, you will have all bases covered in case you choose to use a competitor. Remember, once you select the program whose award you want to receive, *99% of your travel should be with them* if you ever travel. Anytime you have occasion to go away for a weekend or on a short trip, try to use your program and its partners.

There is another bonus for people who own their own business and who travel overseas. A number of foreign airlines such as All Nippon, Japan Air, KLM, Korean and Lufthansa sponsor Corporate frequent flyer programs as well. If you find these programs to be of value, be sure to sign your company up when you enroll yourself. Both you AND your company will receive credit each time you fly. If you happen to own your own company, you will receive double the usual benefits.

## The Dilemma Of Belonging To A Program

When you are shopping for airline fares and call other airlines for their rates, you might discover that the best price is not with your favorite airline or hotel. Sometimes you will have to decide whether you want to save a few dollars more, and sacrifice earning frequent flyer points by flying on a different airline. Unless the savings are substantial, you should consider how much closer the trip would bring you to earning your free ticket. The decision is not easy, particularly when you are close to your goal! If this happens, call your favorite airline back, tell them that you would rather fly with them. Explain that you received a better fare with a competitor. It doesn't always work, but you will sometimes find that they will match the other fare, especially if there is a fare war at that time.

# 10

# USING YOUR PROGRAM

Again, each program is a bit different from the others. Generally, when you receive your statement from the program, you will also receive instructions as to how to redeem your award. Usually, you only have to fill out a form, indicate which of the many free giveaways you want (provided you have enough points), and mail it back to the airline or hotel. Make sure you allow enough time to receive your vouchers prior to your scheduled departure date. These vouchers are normally valid for about one year from the date issued, so don't request them too far in advance.

There have been many abuses of these programs by business travelers over the years, so some airlines place a number of restrictions on their vouchers. Some require you to arrange for your trip directly with them, others allow you to use a travel agent. Some restrict their use to members of your immediate family, others don't mind if you give them to someone else. Many prohibit you from selling them to anyone.

There can also be restrictions on these free tickets. Normally, there are "blackout dates," which means there are certain dates when you cannot use them (for example, during the Christmas, Thanksgiving and Easter holidays). If you are planning to go to Hawaii during the Christmas holidays next year, be sure you know if this period is valid for travel on your free tickets. To avoid disappointment, be sure to check with the program - not when you are ready to request your vouchers, but when you first sign up.

You should also be aware of many special deals which some airline programs offer throughout the year. The airlines are concerned about the large buildup of mileage in player's accounts. To encourage you to redeem some of your accumulated mileage, they have special discount offers or "sales."  For example, 2 free Coach tickets which might normally require 50,000 miles, may be made available for 30,000 miles for a short period of time. Some restrict your travel with these tickets to a limited period - usually in the Fall.

These special sales sometimes permit a cash payment if you don't have enough mileage accumulated. For example, the 2 free tickets noted above might also be offered for 25,000 miles plus a cash payment of $250. These are still super bargains and should not be overlooked. Because of these sales, you should not be in too big a hurry to request your award. Just allow yourself enough time to receive your vouchers for your free tickets. You normally can make your reservations with the airline even if you don't have the voucher in hand. Be sure to tell them that you will be using a frequent flyer award for the trip.

You should also understand that when you travel using free tickets, you normally do not receive credit for the mileage you fly. After all, it is a free trip! On the other hand, if you claim an award which involves a discount (for example, 1 free Coach ticket and 50% off for a companion), you can usually still receive credit. Make sure you ask for the free ticket to be made out in your companion's name, and that the discount voucher is in your own name. Then when you travel on the discount fare, you will still receive credit for the mileage flown.

## Keeping Up To Date

Once you join a program, you will be included in their monthly or bimonthly mailings. These will keep you up to date on your progress in the program with a statement of your activity and about other aspects of the program. You should review your statement carefully. Almost all programs are fully computerized. We all know that even computers make mistakes. Be certain to keep copies of any plane tickets and/or boarding passes as well as any hotel and car rental partner's invoices.

When your statement comes in, check to see if the correct credit (miles or points) was given. Then file your receipts away as you would normally do. If you are using the program's affinity credit card (this will be explained soon), the credit for your usage usually takes a while longer. It takes additional time for the bank to forward its information to the program. Be sure to allow at least 30-45 days for any item to appear, and then call or write asking for your credit. Most of the programs will ask for documentation to be sent in for credit. Above all, you should retain your most recent statement as if it were a bank statement. Don't forget, it is almost as good as money in the bank toward your next free trip.

Be sure to read all the literature you receive from your program. It is not unusual for them to run "specials" for a particular season. Hotels will offer double points for selected locations. Airlines will offer *extra* free tickets if you travel a number of times in a short period, or if you fly from a new airport they are servicing etc. If you can take advantage of these offers, do so. Many enterprising individuals have done this and saved a bundle. For example, an airline may offer a free coach ticket if you fly six times during October and November. Let's say you would like a free ticket to Los Angeles which might normally cost $600. By inquiring about airfares to nearby cities, you might discover there is a $39 fare available to one of them. If you fly 3 round trips to this city (6 trips) for a total cost of $234, you would receive a ticket to L.A. worth $600. Some people have made two or more round trips in a single day! Be certain to follow the program rules carefully. The offer may require that you also fly a certain number of miles while taking your flights, but this is not always true. These special offers are even more generous than the normal program offerings. You will still receive credit in your account for the actual mileage flown as well!

Offers are constantly being made to encourage you to buy non-related items with the enticement of additional points. Subscriptions to The Wall Street Journal and business magazines are often available not only at reduced prices, but with a thousand or so program points offered as a bonus. Purchases from the airline's gift catalog (found in the seat pocket in front of you on the plane) generally earn bonus points based upon the amount you spend. The Northwest WorldPerks program recently sponsored an MCI telephone card, which earns you 1 mile for every dollar you spend making phone calls. They even offered a free upgrade to First class as an extra incentive to sign up for this offer.

If you don't hear from your program on a regular basis, it is probably because you have not earned any points in the current statement period. The airlines especially will eliminate your name from their mailings if you have not been an active player. Just call them up and ask for a copy of their latest bulletin. This is important since you could be missing out on some great opportunities. You will usually not have this problem if you have their credit card, since you will more than likely be using it on a regular basis and receiving credit.

## Extra Bonuses

Many programs have offers from time to time where you receive bonus points if you get someone else to sign up. Usually, the other member has to travel within a certain period of time, or earn a certain number of points within a year to receive your bonus. Don't overlook this opportunity, especially if you know of someone who is going to travel in the near future anyway. Not only will you be doing your friend a favor, but you will also be a few thousand points better off.

Almost all airline and hotel programs give preferential treatment to members of their programs. If there are spare seats available in First class, often these are given to travelers who belong to a program. Hotel programs often grant check cashing privileges, free newspapers, free continental breakfast, no charge for an additional person in your room, free shoe shines and a host of other amenities when you belong to their program. Some hotels will upgrade members to a nicer room without additional cost. Very often, there are special rates available to members of the program which are not available to the public. Unfortunately, sometimes there are so many players flying or staying at a hotel, it is difficult to give everyone special treatment.

Most programs have what could be called a "club within the club." Programs give special recognition to people who travel more than the average player. Airlines have special Bronze, Silver, Gold or Platinum levels which you might be eligible for after flying 25-50,000 miles. Some only include players who are in the top 2-3% of all their members. Once you achieve this level, there are even greater benefits. Some permit automatic upgrades to First class whenever there are seats available. Most give bonus points (usually 10-50%) for any mileage earned. Similar prestige levels in the hotel programs entitle you to stay in a suite for the cost of a standard room. Others reserve special sections or floors in the hotel with special services provided.

# 11

# BUT
# I NEVER
# TRAVEL!

Even if you never board a plane or stay at a hotel or rent a car, there is still a great way to earn thousands of points in your program... or at least in most of the major programs. In fact, you don't even have to leave your home! This is a feature overlooked by most business travelers.

Thousands of people claim their airline or hotel awards without ever seeing an airplane or a hotel room. Even people who are afraid of flying have earned free airline tickets and given them as gifts to friends or relatives. What a great birthday or Christmas present!

As pointed out earlier, these programs have been so successful, everyone wanted to get in to the act. And the banking industry did not want to be left out in the cold. Most of the bigger airline and hotel programs have teamed up with major banking institutions, and are now offering what is called an "affinity card." It is cosponsored by a bank and the airline or hotel program. This is nothing more than a MasterCard or Visa with the name of the program as well as the name of the bank on it.

It is referred to as "affinity" because it is issued by the bank to a group of people who have a common affinity; namely, membership in a frequent flyer or frequent guest program. You may already be familiar with these types of cards - college alumni associations, labor organizations, charitable. organizations and professional sports teams currently sponsor them. When you use other affinity cards, a certain percentage of your purchases are credited to the sponsoring organization. In the case of sports affinity cards, you can earn credits toward team sportswear and game tickets.

The secret to using these cards in conjunction with the airline and hotel programs is that, when you use them, the program credits your account with points for the money you spend. For example, if you charge $245 in May, most programs will credit you with 245 points - as if you had flown on their airline for that many miles! Sorry - most programs don't give you credit for cash advances. Some of these programs will even transfer any balance you have on your present card to theirs. The number of points you receive is a little different for each card. The Marriott program, for example, gives you 3 points for every $1 you spend in their hotel. When you use their affinity card for other purchases, they give you 2 points for every $1 you charge.

In choosing a program to join, you should consider whether a program sponsors an affinity card, and join the program for that reason. Once you join and receive your card, use it regularly to accumulate points toward your free vacation.

## Credit Cards - Other Benefits

Even if you are not interested in one of the affinity cards, you should be certain to have at least one major credit card with you whenever you travel. They are often necessary even if you intend to pay cash for your vacation.

Today, it is very difficult to travel without a major credit card in your wallet or purse. In fact, it is almost impossible to cash a check or rent a car when you are away from home without a card. It is primarily used as a means of identification.

Without an acceptable credit card, most car rental agencies will require a substantial cash deposit which might be several times more than the car will cost for your vacation. Several will not rent to you without a credit card even if you offer to leave a cash deposit equal to the value of the car! You will, of course, receive a refund for any excess deposit to which you are entitled, but you might have to wait for up to a month to get your refund check. When you have an acceptable credit card, use it for identification. When you return the car you can pay cash if you wish. No charges will be made to your credit card.

Hotels generally require cash deposits if you don't have a credit card when you check in. You should also understand hotel policies regarding "guaranteed" rooms. When you make your hotel reservation, you will normally be told that your room will be held only until 6 p.m. on the night you are scheduled to arrive. In resort areas, the time is usually 4 p.m. If you know that you will be arriving later than that time, or if you are not certain, be sure to "guarantee" your room. The hotel will require that you do this with a major credit card over the telephone. This will ensure that when you arrive after 4 or 6 p.m., you will still have a room waiting for you.

If you do not guarantee your reservation, and you arrive late, you may very well find that your reservation was cancelled and your room rented to someone else. If the hotel has no other space available, you will have to start looking for a hotel somewhere else. This can be the beginning of a very disappointing vacation.

On the other hand, if you do guarantee a room, and you fail to show for any reason, the hotel will charge your credit card for the room rate for one night. This is only fair to the hotel, because they will have held that room for you, not knowing if you were going to show up for your room at 3-4 o'clock in the morning. When they hold your room, they may have to turn down business from someone else who is ready to rent it.

If you do guarantee your room, and you later change your travel plans, *be sure to cancel* your reservation well before your deadline. When you guarantee your arrival, most hotels will tell you how much in advance you must to cancel. Be sure to request a confirmation number or a person's name when you cancel a previously guaranteed reservation. If you are later charged for the room, you will have to prove that you cancelled in order to receive a credit.

## Cautions

As with all credit cards, you should be aware of your buying habits and your own financial limitations. Be sure you don't go into debt above your head. Despite a prime rate that remains at about 9-10%, interest rates on ALL credit cards today are extremely high. Affinity cards are no exception! Banks which currently offer these cards to airline and hotel programs are charging as much as 19 percent. If you are not careful about paying your bills on time, the interest can pile up. You do NOT receive points in your program for any interest charged.

If you shop around for a credit card you will find many other MasterCards or Visas with much lower interest rates. But they will not earn you points toward your free vacation. Some programs offer a "regular" card as well as a "Gold" card with a higher credit limit. You will find that one card has a lower interest rate than the other. The Eastern and Continental Airlines' cards, for example, charge an annual interest rate of 19.95% for the "regular" card, and 18.95% for their "Gold" card.

## Additional Advantages

There are a number of additional benefits which come with affinity credit cards which you do not generally receive with your regular bank card. You should certainly consider these benefits before you decide to apply.

First, most programs will give you bonus points for accepting the card. Some will give you credit whether your application is approved or not. When you receive your card, most programs will credit your program account with points the first time you use it. In the case of Eastern Airlines, you get 2500 miles for applying, and another 2500 miles the first time you use it!

Second, there are a number of benefits included with these cards which can be of great value when you travel. Most of these are rather comforting to have when you are away from home: check cashing privileges, emergency cash, emergency airline tickets, huge lines of travel accident insurance (ranging from $100,000 to $500,000), telephone message service while away from home, car rental deductible insurance (ranging from $1-5000), reimbursement for lost luggage (ranging from $1-3000), credit card registration (in case you lose your wallet), and many other benefits. Most of the serious problems you might encounter on a vacation have been anticipated with these benefits.

If you apply for a Gold MasterCard through one of the programs which offer it, not only will you receive a slightly lower interest rate, but you will generally receive an even better benefit package. These may include a legal referral service, a prescription forwarding service (in case you forget your medicine), and increased insurance coverages.

Like standard MasterCard and Visa cards, most of these cards also charge an annual fee, usually around $25-30. As an extra enticement to sign up for these cards, most of the programs will waive the annual fee for the first 6 months, so you only pay 1/2 the annual fee in the first year.

A summary of Affinity Cards which are offered through these giveaway programs is included in Appendix F. At the time of publication, other programs were in the process of creating similar offers, so this list may not be up to date. When you are signing up for a program, be sure to ask the airline or hotel if they have an affinity credit card offer. And, if you feel comfortable with a credit card in your pocket, *then by all means, request one, and increase your points.* If you are uncomfortable with credit cards, remember, you can always pay your balance as soon as the statement arrives, usually without paying interest. Even if you don't want the card, apply for it anyway. Receive your bonus points. Maybe even charge $5 on it to get the second bonus. Then return it to the bank and ask them to cancel your account. You will still be able to keep the bonus points you earned.

## Tips on Using Your Card

Once you receive your credit card, remember that every dollar is worth a point in most programs. One of the nice things about them is that your purchases do not have to be travel related. So when you have dinner, present your card... and earn miles! If possible, try to change your spending habits by charging whenever you normally would pay cash. Promise yourself that you will pay the bill as soon as it arrives.

With a little creativity, you will find many ways to charge things which you never did before. One man arranged with his dentist to pay for his dental work with his MasterCard and received over 2000 free miles. Going to the dentist does not always have to be so painful anymore! You can literally earn a free vacation while you shop. Utilizing The Home Shopping Club and other cable shopping services can now be even more profitable!

When you travel, you can actually collect twice for the same transaction. For example, if you belong to the Marriott Honored Guest program, you receive 100 points for one night in the hotel, plus 10 points for every dollar charged to your room (telephone, room service etc.). If you carry the Marriott First Card, a Visa card, and charge your hotel bill to it, you will ALSO receive 3 points for EACH dollar charged. If you are using an airline card and you charge your airline tickets to it, not only will you earn the normal points for the flight, but you will also receive points equal to the purchase price of the tickets.

Most programs offering these credit cards will issue additional cards for other family members. Be certain to check the credit application and program literature, or call and find out if charges incurred by other family members will count toward YOUR airline or hotel program. When your children are away at college, spending your hard earned money, give them one of your credit cards. You should at least benefit from their carefree spending!

# 12

# OTHER CREDIT CARDS

There are a host of other credit card issuers which offer various travel incentives for using their plastic. There are few which come close to the benefits you can receive by using an affinity credit card as just described. Banks and other credit card issuers are also in a very competitive industry. Recently, a number of them have added travel benefits, and others will be doing the same in the future. Some of these fringe benefits can be very helpful in cutting your vacation costs.

It is virtually impossible to travel without at least one credit card in your pocket. If you are serious about saving money on your vacation, you should consider the benefits of each type of credit card and the relative value of each. If you decide not to use an affinity card, be certain you use one of the following cards. Choose the one which best fits your personal spending patterns, and use it exclusively toward your vacation savings.

## Diners Club

Not to be outdone by its competitors, Diners Club has developed its own program with a number of major airlines and hotels. Once you have applied and been accepted, there is a feature of their card called Club Rewards which you should use. Each time you use your card for travel and entertainment expenses, you receive a point for each dollar charged. These points can be transferred to participating airline and hotel programs, as if you had used their affinity credit card, or as if you had flown with them or stayed at their hotel. By advising Diner's of your account number with an airline or hotel program, the points earned in the Diners' program can be transferred to your favorite program.

Another nice feature is that if you belong to more than one program, you can direct your Diners' credits to whichever program you wish. Airline programs participating in this program are American, Braniff, Continental, Eastern, Northwest, TWA, and United. Hotels programs you can transfer to include Hilton, Inter-Continental, Radisson, Ramada, Sheraton and Stouffer.

The number of points actually transferred to your program has various values depending on the program. 2000 Diners Club points are worth 1000 miles in each of the airline programs above. However, the same 2000 points are worth 200 rewards in the Inter-Continental program, 300 credits in the Stouffer Club Express, 1000 points in the Ramada program, 1500 points in Sheraton, or 2000 points in the Hilton or Radisson programs.

In case you already have enough points in each of your programs, you can also earn free or heavily discounted travel packages directly from Diners. In addition to all this, there are many other benefits including a huge Air Travel Accident Insurance policy which takes effect when you charge your airline tickets with their card.

This card has an annual fee of $55 which is sometimes waived for the first year. When you join one of the airline or hotel programs described earlier, you will sooner or later receive a solicitation from Diners enticing you to apply for their card.

## American Express

While all this has been going on, American Express has not allied itself with any particular program. However, charging your tickets on your American Express Card can result in upgrades to First class if you buy your tickets for Pan Am, Northwest or Air France. Depending on the dollar amount of your purchase, you can receive free companion tickets on Pan Am and US Air, and you can also receive discounts on American. There are also a number of promotional offers with Inter-Continental, Omni and Stouffer hotels. The Delta Airlines Frequent Flyer program recently offered double mileage in their program if you charged your airline tickets with an American Express card.

Using an American Express card when you rent a car can also save you $8-12 per day. They automatically provide you with supplementary insurance covering the rental car. You will not have to accept the CDW (Collision Damage Waiver) optional coverage when you rent. This benefit has recently been extended to holders of their green card.

## The Gold MasterCard

Offered through MasterCard International, this card does not have any particular airline or hotel program's name on it. Instead, they entice you to charge your travel related expenses (airfare, hotel and car rentals) on it. The program is called The Master Plan For Travel and you earn "travel transactions" each time you charge your travel expenses. At each predetermined level, you receive certificates for free or discounted airline tickets on United, hotel rooms from Sheraton and car rentals from Hertz. There are six award levels in their program, based upon the number of transactions which you charge. Each transaction must be over $25. The second level, for example, requires you to charge a total of 10 travel transactions to your card. When you get to that level, you receive $50 off the price of a roundtrip ticket on United, 30% off the cost of your hotel bill if you stay at a Sheraton, and the equivalent of a 50% discount on a weekend rental from Hertz.

## Other Credit Cards

There are over 15,000 banks in the U.S. which offer Visa or MasterCards, and each one tailors its card to its own customers. Dozens of these offer travel agency services, travel rebates, or free travel insurance when you use their card. Some of these rebates amount to about 10% back for hotel bills and 5% for air travel. These rebates can be substantial if you do a considerable amount of travelling.

A number of banks are offering their own versions of "frequent" programs, without becoming true partners of any one airline. Bank of America encouraged the use of its charge cards with free gifts as well as free travel. In their Bonus Breakthrough program, in which you could earn 1 point for every $4 spent, you were able to earn travel awards ranging up to a 15 day trip to China for 25,000 points.

# 13

# TRAVEL AGENTS

Hoping that you have read this book carefully up to this point, you should have already selected your destination and airline program, and have plans for your free (or greatly discounted) airline tickets. Make sure that you read your program literature carefully, and that you are aware of any additional benefits you will receive with your free tickets. It is also quite important to have a good travel agent to work with. Choosing one can be just as important as joining the airline and hotel programs. Whether you have already earned your free or discount tickets from the airlines or not, you should still use a travel agent to help you with your other vacation plans.

Using a good travel agent can be a very important part of your entire vacation. A good travel agent can save you hundreds of dollars on your trip. They can also make the difference between a memorable vacation and a disastrous one. It is important to shop for one, and once you are satisfied with the quality of their service, to use them for all of your trips.

There are some important points about travel agents and travel agencies which you should be aware of. Not everyone can open a travel agency. The owner must have worked as a travel agent for about three years with a recognized agency before setting out on their own. They must be also recognized by at least one sponsoring airline whose ticket stock they will use.

The travel agent is a salesperson for virtually every airline, hotel, cruise line, car rental firm, and sight-seeing attraction throughout the world. One exception - today there are a number of agencies which specialize only in cruises because of the increasing popularity and complexity of this type of vacation. Keeping up to date is not an easy task for a travel agency, considering the number of travel suppliers who want their products sold. It is also quite difficult because of the constantly changing prices for various services. The travel agency regularly receives information on new rates, new destinations, and new airlines and hotels. They receive piles of promotional literature on various destinations and on hundreds and hundreds of vacation packages.

A vacation package is normally put together by a wholesale travel agent or a consolidator. It usually includes airfare, hotel and a car rental. Normally these packages cost quite a bit less than if you were to arrange the same pieces separately. This is because the wholesaler purchases in large volumes, and receives huge discounts, much of which are passed on to you. These are often the same package deals which you will see advertised in your newspapers. Often, the airlines themselves put packages together which include a car and hotel.

About 65% of the more than 30,000 travel agencies in the United States are independently owned and operated. The rest are part of larger travel agency organizations like American Express and Liberty Travel which have enormous computerized operations. But smaller agents also use computers.

Today, almost 95% of all agencies have one or more computer terminals in their office. The computers are part of an airline sponsored system which list flight schedules and prices, not only for the sponsoring airline, but usually for most other airlines as well.

The major systems in use are called SABRE (sponsored by American Airlines), Apollo (United and USAir), System One (Continental and Eastern), PARS (Air Canada, Canadian International, Northwest and TWA) and Datas II (Delta). You should be aware that, if your favorite airline is not a part of one of these systems, there may be a problem in obtaining a reservation or tickets. For example, Southwest Airlines is not a host on any of these systems, and your travel agent may have to call their reservation center directly. The agent may also have some difficulty issuing tickets and/or boarding passes for non-affiliated airlines.

The travel agency does not charge you for its services, although this is gradually changing. When you select your arrangements and purchase your tickets, the travel agency receives a commission from the airline, hotel, car rental firm, cruise line etc. Their commission is usually based on the price you pay. In many instances, they have to wait weeks or months for their check. They often have to wait for you to complete your trip before a commission is calculated. You can see that, unless a travel agency does a large volume of business, it can be very difficult to pay salaries, rent, computer rental fees, etc. Despite this, most travel agents keep a bright, cheerful outlook, and are eager to help you with your vacation plans.

Perhaps the nicest benefit of being a travel agent is the opportunity to take free or greatly reduced price trips. These are not always fun and frolic. Most of the time the trip is a business trip for the agent. They are called familiarization trips, and the purpose is to acquaint the travel agent with airline service, a new hotel, or a geographical area. The idea is that, if the agent is familiar with an area, they will be better able to help you with your planning. Of course they might also be inclined to steer you to these places if you are unsure of where you want to go.

Once the agent understands what type vacation you are looking for, they often can give you helpful advice, having been there themselves. It is not uncommon for an agent to relate first hand stories about the bar in a hotel, to suggest that you avoid an area because of weather at a particular time of year, to discuss the condition of a beach, or even suggest a special dish at a nice restaurant in the area - because they have been there. Some agents seem to have been everywhere!

When they are on these business trips, it's not uncommon for an agent to check out a number of other hotels (other than the one paying for their stay), so that they can get a feel for the various price ranges in the area.

So if you can't afford a luxury hotel, they might be able to suggest an economically priced place in the vicinity. If you are not interested in renting a car, the agent can suggest side trips by bus tour operators. They can even find you a hotel which has limousine service to and from the airport. This type of personal action with an agent can make a big difference and make your trip a truly enjoyable one.

## Selecting a Travel Agent

Everyone should select a travel agent, just as you would choose a family doctor. A reference or recommendation from a satisfied friend is probably the best way to choose one. Convenience of the location, personal acquaintance with an agent, hours of operation, and your prior travel experiences could all have a part in your selection.

Agencies which are members of ASTA (American Society of Travel Agents) or ARTA (Association of Retail Travel Agents) have a professional Code of Ethics to which they subscribe. You should try to find an agent who belongs to one of these two associations. For one thing, they are professionals and, if you should have any problems with an agency, it's possible to call on the association to help resolve your situation.

Once you select an agent, you should be comfortable with them, and be able to communicate your needs to them. If you are not comfortable or if you feel that they are not catering to your needs, try another. If the person you deal with is obviously not experienced either with your type of vacation or your geographical area of interest, ask if someone else in the office is, and talk to that person. If an individual agent has "CTC" after their name, this means they are a Certified Travel Counselor, they have at least 5 years of travel experience and have taken additional courses for credit.

## Dealing With a Travel Agent

Before you go to an agency, you should have a good idea of what you would like to do, when you would like to go, how many people will be travelling with you, how long you can stay, and what your interests will be when you get there (lying on the beach, sight-seeing, golf, tennis, or all of these). If possible, you should have already gone to the bookstore or library and read as much as you can about your destination. Be sure to inquire of friends or relatives who have taken a similar trip about their experiences.

Even if you have no idea what you would like to do or where you would like to get your suntan, an agent can be especially helpful in giving you ideas.

The first thing you should do with the agent is to be honest and explain your situation. Explain if you have earned free or discounted airline tickets or that you have discount vouchers for a hotel or car rental. Explain if you have already checked directly with the airline and obtained a low fare. Be sure to point out if you have already made reservations with the airline. Tell them that you are looking for a cheaper airfare, or that you would like to find an economical hotel in the area, or that you are interested in a particular package you read about in the newspaper. If possible, clip the ad from the paper and bring it with you. Or explain that you are interested in a certain type of vacation and are that you will be open to their suggestions.

Don't hesitate to browse through the travel agent's literature racks looking for trips that might be of interest to you. Be sure to ask if they have any other literature available about your destination. Very often, the agency has so much promotional material available that they cannot display even one tenth of it.

If you are interested in a tour, and you have not seen any of interest in the agent's literature, ask if they have a copy of the "Consolidated Tour Manual." You can review this book to get ideas for your trip. This publication lists almost every tour operated throughout the world by major tour operators.

If you are not concerned about including airfare in your tour package (because you already have your free tickets), ask if they have the Sales Directory of the National Tour Association. This book lists packages for "land only" arrangements which might be of interest to you.

If you have not yet earned your free or discounted trip, be absolutely honest and explain what your budget will be for the entire trip. If money is no object, say so. If you can only afford, say $1200, including air and hotel, mention this and you will only be told about offers within your price range. You will save both yourself and the agent a lot of frustration. If you are purchasing an airline ticket, ask the agent to find you the best price for your favorite airline or one of its travel partners. This will earn you credit in your frequent flyer program. Be certain to ask as well about low fares on other airlines. Then decide which is more important to you. Hopefully your favorite airline will have the lowest price.

## Upgrading Accommodations

You must remember that the agency is working on a commission basis, and will sometimes try to sell you on the idea of upgraded accommodations. These will not only make your trip more luxurious (and expensive), but will also increase their commission checks. For your information, most travel agency employees work on a straight salary, and the agency receives the commissions. Of course, you will be tempted to upgrade to a better tour with better class hotels, to travel on a scheduled airline rather than on a charter to Europe, to take a hotel room with a view of the ocean rather than overlook the parking lot, to rent a luxury car rather than an economy, or to take an outside cabin on your cruise rather than an inside one.

You should consider some of these for practical purposes. If you plan to spend a good deal of time in your hotel room (e.g. on your honeymoon) you might want a nice view. If you are travelling with your mother-in-law and three children and will have plenty of luggage, you will need more trunk space in a larger rental car.

## Understanding The Agency Computer

The airline computer system used by the agency has only a limited number of hotels listed for each destination - usually the higher priced ones. When you begin to talk about your hotel accommodations, don't hesitate to ask the agent if they have looked in some of the handbooks and manuals which are available. These list almost all hotels in an area. Ask them to look at The Official Airline Guide (OAG) Travel Planner or The Hotel and Travel Index, and don't hesitate to ask to look at these books yourself.

In addition to all the other services a travel agent will provide for you, their computer system will help in finding you the best available air fare. Each of the airline systems has a built in low fare finder. The Pars/TWA system actually has two, called the "Low Fare Finder" and "Magic Fare." The American Airlines Sabre system has a bargain finder called "Bargain Finder." System One calls theirs "Quick Quote," while United's is called "Dollar Saver." Make certain that your travel agent uses these or other sophisticated computer programs when they do a search for you.

## Special Travel Agency Programs

The popularity of free travel rewards has not been limited to airline and hotel programs. Some travel agencies have created their own programs because of tremendous competition in that industry. One travel agency sponsored a program where soap wrappers could be redeemed for discount certificates which had to be used at their agency. Obviously, they could be applied to discounted travel as well.

Hundreds of travel agencies around the country have started their own frequent traveler programs. Although geared to the business traveler, these programs are available to anyone who travels with any frequency. McTravel of Deerfield, Ill. and Travel Specialists of New York City are two of the most popular agencies with their own programs.

The International Airline Passengers Association (phone 800-FLY-IAPA) offers a program in which you earn credit for travel booked through their agency. These credits can be redeemed for merchandise when enough points are accumulated.

Other agencies have what is called "Net Pricing" arrangements. Although this is generally offered only to large business customers, some agencies have offered this plan to the public. They have not been too popular because most people don't understand how a travel agency makes money or what net pricing means. An agency makes its money from the airlines, hotels, car rental companies and cruise lines which it books for you. These companies send a check or allow a discount, usually 10-15% of the ticket price. It does not come out of your pocket. The travel companies will not give these commissions to anyone but a recognized agent.

Under net pricing, an agent may sell you a ticket at their cost (ticket price less 15%), but add on a charge of, say, $10 as a handling fee. This is sometimes referred to as wholesale pricing. In this way, you save money and the agent makes a few dollars, although not as much as they normally might.

If you see any advertising for travel agencies which offer discounts off travel packages or which mention net pricing or frequency clubs, be sure to check them out. When searching for a travel agency, ask if they offer net pricing on purchases. If they do, you will have found another bargain.

## Other Travel Agency Services

There are a number of other things which a good travel agent can do to take the hassle out of your trip. While an agent can book you on just about any airline, even if it is not the same as the airline sponsoring their computer system, they can often print your boarding passes. This can be very helpful when you get to the airport since you will not have to wait on long lines just to get your pass. When you select you agent, try to find one who can issue boarding passes for your favorite airline.

An agency often has discount coupons for your destination which can save you money on attractions, meals etc. They can explain how to go about getting your passport, visas or inoculations if any are required. They should be able to explain what type of weather you can expect and what type of clothing to bring. Often they can give you a currency guide for a foreign destination. They can recommend some good guidebooks about your destination. A new selling tool which many travel agencies are now using is the use of video cassettes. So if you want to go to a popular spot like Cancun, chances are that you will be able to see a 15-20 minute film, giving you an idea of what to expect before you go.

Most travel agencies offer trip insurance if you are interested, and many will even recommend and sell you luggage or travel appliances if you require these. And most important, they should explain any restrictions on your tickets, any cancellation penalties which might be involved, and any other fees for which you might be responsible.

## A Final Word About Travel Agencies

It should be no surprise that a travel agency might not be too excited about spending much time with you trying to find reduced fares, while cutting their own commissions. You may find that you will receive one type of reception when you are only shopping, or when you don't know when or where you want to go. When you walk in and tell the agent you are ready to do business, you will get an entirely different reception. As in any other business, time is money. Some travel agencies are finding that it is not worth their effort to deal with onetime customers or people who want extremely detailed itineraries planned. Some agencies are beginning to charge small fees for their services. These fees are well worth it if the agent is able to save you additional money. It's worth spending $10 any time you can save $50!

Remember that the travel agent is only making your arrangements for you. They are not responsible for your having a great time or for the weather while you are away. They have no control over luggage being lost by the airline, the hotel giving you a room near the pinball machine, or your rented car getting a flat tire. Believe it or not, some people have actually brought lawsuits against travel agents because the hotel gave them a suite rather than a single room when they arrived! If any of these things happen and blemish your trip, take up your problem with the airline or hotel. And be sure to let the travel agent know about it. Next time, they might not recommend that supplier to another customer.

# 14

# CONSOLIDATORS

From time to time, while reading newspaper travel advertisements, you will notice what appears to be almost unbelievable prices to Europe, South America, Africa and Hawaii. Some outstanding deals are offered for cruises and tours as well. Occasionally, there will be exceptional prices within the U.S. These ads are not placed by the airlines, but by firms referred to as wholesalers, consolidators, bucket shops or discounters. There are several methods by which these firms operate, and these will be discussed below. It is important to understand where these tickets come from, how you can locate these firms and how they operate, so that you can take maximum advantage of them and save even more money.

## How They Operate

Some of these companies purchase huge quantities of airline tickets and hotel rooms at very low prices and, in turn resell them. Sometimes they purchase tickets overseas using foreign currency to save additional money. Other times they purchase airline tickets from other businesses through barter organizations. There are times when an airline will sell tickets to a discounter, particularly when their own sales are not going as well as expected. The airlines believe that it is better to fly with the plane full, and collect something for every seat on the plane, than to fly only half full. These tickets are then offered to you. The consolidator often combines these tickets into a tour package which you may purchase from almost any travel agency. When the time approaches for departure, and they find there are still unsold tickets on hand, they very often offer these tickets directly to the public. In almost every situation, the price you receive will normally be much below any price you will ever receive directly from an airline or a travel agent.

Many of these firms only handle airline tickets for a particular part of the world, specializing in Europe or Asia. Some consolidators will deal directly with the public and advertise in newspapers. Some will do business with you but do not advertise. Others deal only with travel agencies. Many consolidators will try to accommodate you with any reasonable request. For example, if you are aware of a particular package (even an escorted tour), ask if they can obtain it for you. If they do not have it available, they will often try to find it for you - at a better price than you would normally pay.

## Dealing With A Consolidator

By the time you call a consolidator, you should have a good idea of the standard full fare prices to your chosen destination. When you call, be specific as to when you want to travel, but keep your plans open to other dates as well. It is always an advantage to be flexible in your planning. Remember that if you are going overseas, your flight will depart from a major airport on the East or West coast. It will be your responsibility to get to that airport. The consolidator will normally not be able to help you with this.

Consolidators very often will offer to sell tickets on charter flights (see Chapter 16). Some charter lines are quite good, while others are not quite as reliable. If you are comfortable with the price and you are aware that it is a charter flight, by all means purchase it.

Besides great cost savings, there are a number of other benefits in dealing with consolidators. Under existing airline rules for certain types of fares like the APEX, tickets must be purchased a certain number of days prior to the trip. Often, you will find that a consolidator will waive this restriction and sell you this fare a few days before scheduled departure. You only have to allow enough time to have the tickets delivered to you.

Sometimes you can find a one way ticket for just half the cost of a round trip ticket. Normally a one way fare costs about 60-75% of the price of a round trip ticket. If you are a gambler, you could purchase a low priced one-way ticket to Europe, and try to find a bargain ticket home. There are hundreds of very popular bucket shops in Europe. Most of them are located in London and advertise heavily in local newspapers. Most offer one-way tickets back to North America.

Perhaps the biggest advantage in dealing with consolidators is that you will find discounts on First and Business class. These are not generally available anywhere else, even from the airlines. This is particularly beneficial for people who like to travel in style without paying full price. Very often, you will be able to buy a discounted First class ticket for less than the full fare cost of a Coach seat. When you call, you can request a particular airline affiliated with your frequent flyer program. As a bonus, you usually receive double mileage in your program when you fly in First class. If you are not able to obtain a Coach ticket and the discounter has only First class available, try bargaining with them for a better price. Often they will bring their price down somewhat if they feel that you are ready to buy. When you find a fare you are satisfied with, be prepared to pay for the tickets with your credit card over the telephone. This is the only way most will do business. In any event, the tickets you buy will give you the same rights as if you had purchased them directly from the airline.

There are some substantial savings available if you follow the steps below:

1 - Watch the Sunday travel section of your newspaper for companies which advertise these unbelievable fares. In time you will recognize those who repeat week after week. This is generally a good indication of a successful and popular firm.

2 - Compare the rates they offer to the best rates you can obtain on your own.

3 - Some advertisers do not have a great reputation in this field. Some firms (which will be covered in Chapter 19) have posed as legitimate consolidators. At times their prices may seem too good to be true. If there is any question in your mind about their legitimacy, check with your travel agent and ask if they are aware of the reliability of the advertiser. Or call the Better Business Bureau in the city where they are located to determine if there have been any problems with this firm.

4 - Call and ask if they have any literature available for the tickets or tour packages offered. If there is adequate time available before your trip, they should send you a full description.

5 - Make sure the price offered is for a round trip. Ask if there will be any additional charges required either for their processing, when you get to the airport, or payable to the airline. Some operators also have a surcharge for credit card transactions. Basically, be certain you know what your final cost will be.

6 - If there are any additional purchases required, cease all further conversations with the supplier. Several deceptive firms have offered bargain rates (example: New York to Hawaii for $29) and require you to purchase at least 7 nights in a luxury hotel. This could cost you more than the full fare for the plane tickets alone.

7 - Sometimes you will be asked to pay for your tickets before the airline or flight number can be confirmed. In this situation, the discounter may be waiting for additional seats from an airline. This just might never happen. You could receive a phone call a few days before your trip, only to be told that your opportunity has vanished ... sorry! Stay away from any situation where you are not confirmed on a particular airline and flight number.

8 - When you do make a purchase, call the airline and/or hotel and verify your reservations. Make sure there are no additional charges required.

9 - Ask how you will receive your tickets. Most will use UPS or the U.S. Mail, and most firms charge a nominal price for this delivery. Refuse to do business with anyone who requires a cash payment.

When you locate a good consolidator, you can save hundreds or thousands of dollars on your vacation.

# 15

# TRAVEL CLUBS

You may have heard about travel clubs or you may already belong to one. These organizations charge you an annual fee to belong to their club, and offer discounted airline tickets and tour packages, usually at short notice. Some have a phone number which you can call to learn of the latest travel bargains available. Others send out brochures every week or once a month. Most only offer you those trips which they know will sell out quickly, so you may not have as wide a selection as you would like.

Most clubs have a range of other services and benefits available to their members. Discounts on hotels and car rentals are common, but generally are not much better than the discount you would receive as a member of a frequent flyer or frequent guest program. Some offer a plan where you receive credit for a percentage of the amount you spend with them. This credit can be applied later against the cost of another trip booked through their club.

Travel clubs often, if not always, purchase their tickets and tours from the same wholesalers and consolidators mentioned in the last Chapter. They then add on enough to cover their own operating costs and a profit. These clubs can offer a great deal of savings to those who are not adventurous enough or who choose not to deal directly with a consolidator. These clubs are very popular with people who like to take frequent weekend or short trips. They are particularly appealing to singles and couples without children who can travel at a moment's notice. It is not very common to find bargain prices for trips more than a month or two in advance. If you would like to be certain of your plans well before your vacation, a travel club may not be the right choice for you.

When you deal directly with a consolidator, you may have more flexibility and more variety. And you save the annual travel club fee and mark up which the travel club has to add on.

Recently, Eastern Airlines began its own version of a travel club. Known as the Weekender's Club, it offers highly discounted roundtrip airfares and tour packages to its members. There is an annual fee to participate which ranges from $100 for a single person, to $175 for a couple's membership. Offerings to popular destinations are made each week after the airline evaluates available space. Rather than fly with an empty seat, they offer their members tickets at bargain prices. These are usually available only on short notice. This club has become so popular that you can probably expect to see other airlines begin their own versions soon.

Before you join a travel club, you should evaluate how often you think you will be able to get away for a weekend in addition to your annual vacation. You should also consider whether your annual fee can be recovered through the savings offered.

# 16

# OTHER COST SAVING IDEAS

## Charter Flights

In the past there were a large number of charter airlines in the U.S. offering very attractive fares, especially on flights going overseas. With the heavy competition among scheduled airlines in recent years, it is difficult to find charters easily, and when you do, the savings are not that dramatic.

There have been a number of problems with charter flights in the past. Full payment must often be made several months in advance. You often have to check in 2-3 hours before the flight, and because of the limited number of agents available, there are usually long waiting lines. The planes generally are more crowded than usual, and the meals, if there are any, are often simply a box lunch. Over the last 5-10 years, a number of charter airlines have gone out of business after collecting payment from passengers. It has been quite difficult to obtain refunds from them under these circumstances. Be certain to check with your travel agent about the airline and its reputation before you buy one of these tickets, regardless of the great price you may obtain.

Charters are still very popular in Europe where competitive rates are not as common. Check with your travel agent about foreign charter flights, or better still, check with a travel agent after you arrive in Europe. There are quite a few charter airlines in Europe offering great deals on trips to other European countries. You could use these for a side trip on your vacation. You can also check with consolidators (see Chapter 14), which very often have discount tickets available for charter flights.

## Fly Somewhere Else

Because of the fierce competition by airlines, fares to major cities are often lower than to smaller outlying cities. If you are travelling to a smaller city, be sure you also check on the price of a ticket to a nearby major airport. If you insist on flying into the smaller city, you will probably have to change planes in the nearby major airport anyway. You will probably fly on a small regional airline to your final destination. Very often it is much cheaper to fly into a major city and rent a car. When you arrive at your destination, return the car to the airport you originally wanted to go to. You can also take a bus from the major airport to the smaller city. This minor inconvenience can easily save you $100-300.

## Travel In The Off-Season

Airlines, hotels, cruise lines and car rental companies frequently have different rates for various "tourist" seasons. This is in response to normal supply and demand. In the busier months, when thousands of people are going to an area because its popularity or because of better weather, travel companies can charge just about anything they want. This is called "peak" season. Some people will be willing to pay full price for this time period. The "off-peak" season can be defined as the time of year when fewer people want to travel to a destination. In between these two seasons is a period referred to as the "shoulder" season. The change from one season to the next is literally overnight.

As soon as a season is officially over, rates tumble by as much as 30-60% For example, a good hotel room at a popular ski resort might cost $150 or more per night during the peak season. This is because avid skiers are willing to pay top dollar for prime time. But on April 1st the rates might be slashed to $55-60 per night. This rate reduction does not mean there will be no skiing available. For a few weeks before and immediately after the very best skiing, there is a period when conditions might be considered very good. If you are interested in a particular location but not willing to pay top dollar, you should seriously consider travelling in the off-season. A similar situation occurs in almost every popular tourist destination in the world.

Peak season in Florida is in winter, but rates fall off drastically after April 1. Australia is similar, with off-peak ranging from April through September; but, you must remember that the seasons are quite the opposite of our seasons in the Northern Hemisphere. Off peak in Mexico and the Caribbean ranges from late April through mid-December. Late summer and early fall is the best time to find good bargains on cruise lines. Europe is generally very crowded during July and August. Just about any other time, rates are lower and the crowds will be much smaller. You may have noticed that when a popular destination is off-season, it does not necessarily mean that the weather will be bad. May and June are delightful months in the Caribbean.

Not only can you benefit by saving a substantial amount of money, but you should also have a lot more peace and quiet when you visit typical tourist attractions. You will often find that service at a hotel will be much better in the off-season since the help will not be quite as busy. They will have had a chance to recover from the crowds of the peak season.

It is often true that the more luxurious the hotel, the more the rates drop in the shoulder or off-peak seasons. It's important to know about the dramatic drop in rates, because you should seriously consider making a slight change in your travel plans to take advantage of these terrific savings. Keep in mind that it's always off-season somewhere. You can always take advantage of reduced prices if you are willing to be somewhat of an adventurer.

## The Corporate Discount

Most airlines have avoided giving discounts on tickets to corporations, but there have been a large number of exceptions over the last year or two. Today, hundreds of major U.S. companies receive 5-15% off all tickets they purchase. Often the airlines give a special rate on flights to certain cities where a company may have a large plant, or where seminars or conventions are often held. If this city also happens to be your destination, you might be able to obtain the same rate. If you work for a large company, be certain to check with the travel department to determine if they can get a better fare for you. Very often, as a courtesy to its employees, large corporations will accommodate you and pass on any discounts they receive.

## Senior Citizen Discounts

Most airlines will not give a senior citizen a discount simply for attaining a certain age as many hotels will. Northwest and United offer a 10% discount to people over 62. There may be certain restrictions in order to receive these discounts however. Other airlines may have similar offers. There are also a number of special clubs established by many airlines which afford a number of opportunities for discounts. These normally require an annual fee, and the benefits range from discounts on certain classes of tickets to unlimited travel. When you call for reservations or to join an airline frequent flyer program, be sure to ask about these programs.

## Keep Up To Date On The Travel World

There are many situations where choice airline tickets are available and ultimately go unused because a buyer cannot be found. Most are sold for substantially less than the best bargains available directly from the airline.

If you are serious about saving on your vacation costs, one of the most important things you can do is to keep up to date on the travel world. Read everything you can get your hands on related to travel. It is important to read a daily newspaper, or better, the Sunday Edition of a major metropolitan area paper. Some papers have columns or entire sections about travel. If possible, obtain a copy of the Sunday New York Times which has a travel section as large as the entire newspaper in some cities. Copies of the Times are often available at your public library if you cannot purchase one locally. Other papers with exceptionally good travel sections are the San Francisco Examiner, The Los Angeles Times and The Chicago Tribune.

When you are finished with the sports section or local news, be sure to read everything about the major airlines, hotels and car rental companies in the business section. Keep posted on any developments about new programs and promotions, particularly about your selected airline and its program. Many times, special promotions offered by your program are announced to the press weeks before you will receive your statement. This news may have an impact on the rates the airlines will be charging in upcoming months. It might also have an effect on your strategy for achieving your free ticket goal. Don't overlook news articles about local travel agents either. They can be your best friend as you have just learned.

If you skip over the "Personals" section, you may have missed one of the best opportunities for finding bargains. Because of the many restrictions which airlines have placed on their tickets, especially the Supersaver fares, you cannot receive a refund on your ticket if you decide to cancel for any reason. Miss the flight and you lose everything. People who find themselves in this predicament often resort to placing an ad in the Personals section of a newspaper, offering their otherwise worthless tickets for sale.

Some newspapers have a separate section in the classified section for "Air Travel." A recent midweek edition of The Los Angeles Times had 46 different ads to buy or sell tickets at substantially reduced prices. The Dallas Morning News lists airline bargains under "Tickets" in their classified section. If the destination is in line with your plans, and if you have some flexibility, call and make an offer. You should already know the value of the ticket from your research. The seller will probably be willing to take a small loss rather than forfeit the total cost of their ticket.

Normally there is not much problem with using a ticket in someone else's name. The airlines generally don't request identification. However, it is a good idea to at least make certain, if you are a male, that your ticket does not read "Mrs." On the other hand, there can be serious problems when the ticket is a free ticket. Be sure to look at the ticket carefully and see that there was a cash payment made for it.

You should NEVER purchase a ticket in another person's name for a flight to another country. When you arrive at the airport, or later when you arrive in a foreign country, you will be asked for your passport or other identification. Your ticket to another country must be in your own name or you could find yourself in a very embarrassing position. Some people have been denied entry into a foreign country because of this oversight.

## Coupon Brokers

Some of the personal ads you see may have been placed by coupon brokers. These firms purchase free airline awards from business travelers. The frequent business traveler very often earns more free tickets than they know what to do with. The last thing they may want to do on their vacation is to get back on a plane and travel somewhere. They may have been travelling most of the year and simply want to spend a little time at home on their vacation. In order to raise some spare cash, they often sell their awards to a broker. During the last 10 years, more than 50 brokerage firms have come into existence. They purchase these free trip vouchers and resell them to the public and travel agents.

Many of the frequent flyer programs are not concerned with what a player does with an award once it is issued. Some programs prohibit their sale. Over the last few years, a few airlines (particularly American, TWA and United) have gone to war with these brokers, taking them to court. They have put some of them out of business for selling coupons which could not be sold according to the program rules.

If you locate a broker which has a ticket you can use, you can save thousands of dollars, especially on First class tickets. It's not unusual to purchase a First class ticket for less than a full fare Coach ticket to the same destination. And you get to travel in style. Because of the sensitivity of the airlines however, you should be aware that using a free ticket in another person's name could result in the airline not honoring your ticket. So if you deal with a coupon broker, be sure to determine that you will travel in your own name. Remember, many programs allow this. Travelling in someone else's name could be embarrassing and costly to you if the airline suspects that anything underhanded is happening. A simple call to the airline explaining the circumstances and type of ticket should resolve whether the ticket is transferable or usable by someone other else.

Coupon brokers often advertise in the travel sections of Sunday newspapers. You can usually find them offering to purchase frequent flyer coupons in the classified section of The Wall Street Journal and in USA Today. USA Today has a classified Travel Directory which recently had 22 advertisements from firms offering to purchase airline awards and coupons. What they buy, they must sell!

Heavy travel volume frequently results in overbooking on some flights by the airlines. This results in some people being "bumped" off a flight. When this happens, the airline gives the bumped passenger a voucher worth $200-400. These coupons are often sold to a broker.

The brokers are often aware of which flights are most crowded and wait at the airport to purchase these coupons on the spot. When you locate a coupon broker, be sure to ask if they have any transferable travel vouchers for sale.

You can often buy these at less than face value. For example, a $300 voucher might be sold for $225, and then applied later (for the full $300 - a $75 savings) toward the value of a bargain priced ticket.

If you know someone who travels a great deal of the time, they might be willing to sell or give you one of their awards rather than deal with a broker. Relatives or in-laws who travel frequently might be willing to give you free tickets if their program permits transfers to relatives. Some programs only permit transfer of awards to relatives with the same surname.

## Do Someone Else's Flying

Most airline programs will not credit you for flying in another person's name. However, there is one little known way to fly for free or almost free, and still receive credit in your frequent flyer program. In fact, the price is generally so good that you should not even be concerned with earning points. A number of companies, usually in larger metropolitan areas on the East and West coasts are in the courier business. They transport stocks, bonds and other valuable documents and materials all over the country and throughout the world. Most of their activity is to Europe and Asia. While they have regular employees who do this for a living, there is often a need for additional help.

You will seldom see advertisements for these firms. Look in the Yellow Pages of your telephone book under "Air Courier Service" for a list of them. Or visit your library and examine the phone directories for larger cities. Also look for listings of domestic and international air couriers under "Messenger Service."

Contact one of them and, if you are extremely flexible and willing to travel alone, you can generally arrange to be notified when their need arises. Usually you will be asked where you want to go. They will advise you when they have a need for someone to travel to that destination. Some firms charge a nominal amount for these tickets.

You normally do not receive much advance notice. Since you will be transporting their materials, you will have to check their baggage through and carry your own on to the plane with you. You will need to travel light considering the airline's new restrictions on carry-on baggage. When you arrive at your destination, you will have to claim their baggage and meet with one of their representatives to sign over the package you escorted. Then you will be free to do whatever you want.

Most of the time the courier service will purchase an APEX ticket which requires you to stay for at least 7 days. If you want to see Europe, you will need at least that much time. A round trip ticket is usually provided by the courier. It's not a bad way to see the world for free or next to nothing!

If you want to travel with someone else and there is only one assignment, they will have to make their own arrangements for tickets. One reminder - doing this at the last minute can result in paying a higher fare than normal. You have to remember that, on average, you will be saving 50% on the price of two seats.

If the courier puts you on an airline and you belong to that airline's program, you will receive the frequent flyer points for the trip as well. Be sure to ask if you can choose the airline you will fly on. If possible, select your favorite airline or one of its travel partners for your flight. The courier will usually try to obtain the best priced ticket without regard to your airline preference, or without consideration of your frequent flyer affiliations. If you decide to take advantage of courier service, you might want to sign up for as many programs as possible. In this manner you will receive credit regardless of the airline you fly.

The courier might explain that you are not eligible for frequent flyer points for tickets which they purchase. They really cannot prevent you from doing this. If you are not able to include your account number on the ticket before you fly, be certain to make a photocopy of the ticket and boarding pass. When you return home, send these to the program's headquarters and request credit to your account.

## Do Someone Else's Driving

If you would like to take a trip by car but you don't have one, or if you would prefer not to drive your own car, or if you would like to drive somewhere and return home by air, there is a simple solution. Drive someone else's car. You are not being encouraged to steal a car, but to use one legally. There are a number of ways to do this.

One easy way is (again) to read your newspapers more carefully. In the Personals section, you will frequently see ads requesting someone to "drive my car" to California, or Florida, or wherever. In other cases, someone will be driving a long distance and will be looking for a rider to share expenses. There are many different ways this can work. Normally, you pay for the gas and the owner allows more than enough time for you to get to your destination. You are usually allowed a certain number of miles to get there. Anything over that amount may cost you 5 or 10 cents per mile. Insurance is usually provided by the owner. Be certain to discuss these issues with the owner before you agree to do this, particularly concerning insurance coverage.

Another way to accomplish this is to contact a company which arranges this service. You will probably only find these in the largest cities. Look in the Yellow Pages under "Automobiles - Transporters & Driveaway Companies." These firms arrange with individuals or companies to move cars around the country. Often a bank needs to relocate a repossessed car, or a company will need to move a transferred employee's car. After you tell them where you want to go and when you want to return, they will do their best to accommodate you in both directions.

Don't count on a return trip though. Except for the very largest companies, it's quite difficult to match up both ends of the trip unless you have lots of flexibility. Normally, you will receive the first tank of gas free, and you will have to pay for the rest. You may also have to leave a deposit of $100-150 to cover the cost of any damages you might cause. The deposit will be refunded if you return the car as expected. If you are really lucky, you might be able to arrange to transport a motorhome or recreational vehicle, and save even more on lodging costs along the way.

Another way to drive for free is to contact several car rental companies in your area. Very often, a car from another state or city arrives, and for one reason or other cannot be rented back to its originating city. The larger car rental companies have crews of people who do this on a regular basis and may not be able to help you. However, you may be able to work something out with some of the smaller companies.

Be sure that you are perfectly clear when you call, and do not give them the impression that you "need" a car to go from point A to point B. Otherwise they will consider you a paying customer. When you call the larger car rental companies, do not call their toll-free reservation numbers or their headquarters. Call the local office and ask for the Car Control department. Ask if there are any opportunities to "deadhead" or "nonrev" a car going to a particular city. Both of these terms imply that there will be no charge. Most of them will even pay expenses including tolls and gas. Others may require you to pay for some expenses except repairs.

## Take A Bump

The airlines have learned over the years that a certain percentage of people who make reservations will not show up for the flight. In anticipation of this, they often overbook a flight. Occasionally their estimates are wrong. This requires the airline to "bump" some passengers off the flight. This is not necessarily a major problem to most people. The airline will place those people on another flight, either with another airline or on a later departure. *In addition,* they will issue a voucher worth $200-400 for future travel. This is called "compensation for denied boarding" in official airline jargon.

This can be an extremely rewarding situation, especially when the cost of the original ticket might be extremely low. If you are faced with the opportunity to be bumped, you should seriously consider volunteering by advising the ticket agent of this. Be certain that it is not too late in the day, or you might find yourself stranded overnight while waiting for the next flight out. The earlier you volunteer, the better chance you have of being compensated for your trouble. Pay attention to the activity at the agent's desk, and if there are any signs of overbooking, get ready to move.

Some people with spare time on their hands have made a hobby out of being bumped by the airlines. They spend time at the airports on Mondays and Fridays when the airports are busiest, and observe which flights are often overbooked. Later on, they purchase tickets for those flights. Then they wait at the airport to see if there will be an overcrowded situation, and volunteer to be bumped. If they are bumped, they collect a coupon. If the situation is not favorable, they simply do not present their ticket. Instead, if they expect another overcrowded flight, they return to the ticket counter and change their reservation for the same flight on another day or time. One catch to this scheme is that they must purchase full fare, non-discounted tickets to avoid the restrictions on most other fares. This is usually not much of a problem because, after they collect a number of vouchers for being bumped, they ask for a refund on their original ticket.

# 17

# WATCH
# FOR
# BARGAINS

There are a number of opportunities available - even in advertisements which might otherwise be of no interest to you. Often, you will hear of special offers for airline fares on the radio or TV. Some programs have been so successful that airlines have only run an ad once in a newspaper, and then did only low key promoting in a department store or supermarket. What you normally consider junk mail may also present some valuable opportunities.

The following are examples of some great money saving promotional offers made over the last year or two. There are sure to be many more like these in the future, since each of these were very well received.

## Supermarket Bargains
*   New York Air (now part of Continental) offered a promotion in conjunction with Skippy peanut butter. If you purchased four 18 ounce jars (or larger), and sent in proofs of purchase, you received a free ticket for a

travelling companion. This was equivalent to a 50% discount for two people.

- Ralston cereals (which includes Chex, Fruit Islands, Sun Flakes and Cookie Crisp) ran a "Kids Fly Free" promotion. With five proofs of purchase, you could have received a free round trip ticket on Piedmont Airlines for children travelling with a paying adult. This offer was promoted on TV, radio, and on cereal boxes as well. They also had an instant winning opportunity on game cards inside each box.

- Nabisco Shredded Wheat ran a promotion allowing you up to $25 off the price of a TWA ticket. You had to submit five game cards which were included in the cereal boxes.

- Gillette Razor's promotion with Continental Airlines offered a free companion ticket providing one person bought a full-fare ticket. You had to submit four proofs of purchase for 10-packs of razor blades. Even if you didn't need razors, you could have thrown them away and used the coupon for your own vacation. This was equivalent to a 50% discount.

- Supermarkets continue to be one of the biggest promoters of reduced cost travel, not only by offering merchandise, but also by sponsoring their own programs. From time to time your local store may entice you to collect trading stamps or otherwise arrange to track your purchases (with a shopper ID card), for which you can claim awards. Very often, the award catalog contains discounts on travel suppliers. With these types of promotions, you may have to choose between a 25% discount on airline tickets and a new crock pot! There should be no second thoughts about what you should choose.

## Other Shopping Bargains

- K Mart department stores offered a rebate program where you simply submitted your travel receipts as proof of purchase. You had to use certain airlines, car rental companies, and hotels, and you had to book your travel through a specified travel agency. A short time later, you received a Gift Certificate for use in their stores. These were equal to about 5% of the value of the travel. Not all savings are received directly from the airlines. After all, receiving a cash rebate after your trip is also a savings.

- Computerland had a nationwide promotion that, for purchases of about $3-4000, would give you a free round trip ticket on Eastern Airlines.

- A combined TWA and Polaroid promotion offered a coupon good for 25% off the price of any TWA ticket. This offer required the purchase of certain types of cameras. The coupons were even good for international travel which meant that you could save hundreds of dollars off the price of a ticket to Europe. This program became so popular that Lufthansa, which was not involved in the promotion, eventually began to honor these coupons, apparently because they were losing too much business to TWA.

- Polaroid and Pan Am sponsored a promotion where, if you purchased a Polaroid Spectra camera and a round trip ticket on the Pan Am Shuttle (between New York and Boston or Washington, D.C.), you would receive another free round trip ticket for the Shuttle. This was in addition to other merchandise certificates you could receive for related camera supplies.

## Other Great Offers

- The AT&T Opportunity Calling program, in which you received credit based upon your long distance bills, offered a number of discounts on hotels and airline fares.

- American Express mailed an offer to about a million of its members, enticing them to sign up other people. If you could get three friends to apply for a card and their credit was approved, you earned a free round trip ticket to London on British Airways.

- Continental Airlines announced a special $99 one way fare from New York to Honolulu for a very limited time. The available flights were sold out within 12 hours of the public announcement. A word to the wise - if you hear of one of these "too-great-to-be-true" promotions offered directly by an airline, don't waste time. Grab it! You usually will have a few months to use these tickets. And if you are not able to use them yourself, perhaps someone you know would like to buy your tickets.

  Be sure to carefully read chapter 19 which deals with other "too-great-to-be-true" offers which you should AVOID at all costs!

- Banks have often offered travel rewards for depositing certain amounts into new accounts. For each of these you would earn bargain airfare certificates. These certificates were good for a one way trip anywhere within the 48 States for only $89. Other banks have offered vacations worth $200-1000 for renewing a CD, but with a slightly lower interest rate. These can work in your favor since you will have less interest to report on your income taxes. And the trip you receive (instead of the higher interest) might not be reportable on your tax return. Be sure to check with your tax accountant on the proper handling of these type of free trips.

- Because of the bad press it was receiving about on-time arrivals, Continental Airlines ran a number of newspaper advertisements, and included a "report card" which you had to clip out of the paper. When you flew during a certain time period and reported on your satisfaction with their service, you were sent a check ranging from $10 - 50. The rebate was based upon how much you paid for your ticket.

- American Airlines recently held a "super vacation market" for a weekend in the Dallas area to promote their vacation packages. These packages were sold at from $50-100 off the normal prices.

## Very Special Airline Offers

You just never know what kind of promotion the airlines are going to come up with. In 1987, Delta began to offer double miles (twice the normal earned points) in its program when their tickets were purchased with an American Express card. To retaliate, first one airline, then virtually all the others, began to offer triple miles in their programs. This meant that, once you took a round trip (or a certain number of trips) during a specific period, they would credit you with three times the normal mileage earned. Some of them will be awarding triple miles throughout 1989! This made it three times easier to achieve your free ticket goal. On occasion, some programs offered other opportunities to get in on the triple mileage bonanza. These occurred when the airline wanted to bring attention to a new route or new city it was servicing.

The ramifications are still being felt. In early 1989, the three major Canadian airline programs began offering members of their programs up to six times the normal mileage for flying on their airlines.

# 18

# ADVANCED SAVINGS TECHNIQUES

There are a number of tricks you can use to take advantage of airline ticket pricing, but they must be very carefully planned. These are not for novices or occasional travelers. If you travel more than three or four times a year, and if you are comfortable using airline schedules and their reservation systems, you should consider trying the following techniques.

## Airline Hubs

During the last ten years, the airlines have changed the way they do business. Previously, most flights went from one city to another, and then turned around and flew back again. This was not very profitable. Currently, most major airlines depend on what is referred to as "hubs." Picture the spokes of a wheel with a hub at the center. Airlines have arranged the cities to which they fly in a similar pattern, and have created hubs at major cities in the center. Hubs are basically locations where you get off one plane, walk to another gate, and board another plane going to your ultimate destination.

In this manner, the airlines are able to fill up their aircraft on each flight, rather than have every flight to each destination only half filled. The obvious disadvantage to this arrangement is that you frequently have to change planes in the middle of your trip. This has led to additional travel time of one or two hours for most people.

One advantage of this concept is that you frequently will have a greater choice of destinations to which you can fly. For example, prior to the hub concept, it might not have been possible to fly directly from Akron, Ohio to West Palm Beach, Florida. The only choice you might have had for a Florida vacation without taking another airline was Miami or Orlando. Now, through the use of hubs, you might be able to choose from almost 20 different cities in Florida. Airlines are now able to offer more frequent shorter trips from your city to a hub city, and then from this hub to your ultimate destination. This also works in your favor because you now have a greater selection of departure times to choose from. It also affords you with additional opportunities for flexibility in your planning. When you are shopping for the best fares (see Chapter 4), you have a greater choice of flights on which you might obtain a lower fare.

This concept of connecting flights through hub airports now accounts for 50-75% of all domestic flights. The balance are called nonstop or "through" flights. The airlines still operate direct or nonstop service between cities whenever there is enough passenger volume to justify it. Therefore, New York to Los Angeles or Chicago to Miami nonstop service will probably always be available on major airlines. An airline may also offer one-stop or "through" service to major cities. This entails a stop in another city to pick up additional passengers. The flight then continues to the final destination without your having to change planes. In this situation, you would have stopped at a hub or an intermediate city.

You should be aware of this trend. When you reserve a flight, you should know whether it will be a direct nonstop, or whether you will have to make a connection with another flight. This can be important to you, especially if you are travelling with small children, if you are incapacitated in any way, or if you just dislike changing planes. It's too late to find out when you arrive at the airport that your flight from Los Angeles to New York will involve a change of planes (and maybe an additional hour) in Denver. Sometimes changing planes is more than simply walking to another gate. You might have to go to another terminal building. If making a connection appears to be a problem for you, try to book a nonstop or through flight.

This problem can be even more complicated when weather may be a factor in the connecting city. Changing planes in Denver might be welcome in June, but could be disastrous in January during a heavy snow storm. Bad weather at the connecting city can result in excessive flight delays. You could even find yourself stranded overnight because your connecting aircraft was unable to land at all! Understanding this concept is also very important if you wish to go on to advanced techniques in saving on your airfare.

## Hidden Cities

There are times when you might actually want to connect through a hub or another city and save 30 to 50% off the cost of your airfare. This tactic is best used by people who have some experience in travelling. First time or novice travelers should not attempt this. It is referred to as "Hidden City Ticketing." The airlines frown on the practice, and you will find that travel agents are divided about equally for and against this practice.

Before explaining the technique, you should understand a bit more about airline ticket pricing. If all airlines priced their tickets at their actual cost, virtually everyone would pay the same amount for a ticket on every airline operating between two cities. As explained earlier, airlines react to their competitor's prices more than to their own costs. Profitable or not, they price a ticket to match the other lines.

Sometimes the cost for a ticket to a destination is priced far higher than it should be - at least in relation to the cost of tickets to other destinations. An example is the cost of a full fare Coach ticket from New York to Dallas which might cost about $680 round trip. The cost of a round trip ticket from New York to Oklahoma City (an additional 200 miles) on the same airline might only be about $400. The ironic thing is that in order to go to Oklahoma City, you have to make a connection in Dallas. In Dallas you get off, change planes, and continue your flight on to Oklahoma City. And this costs you less! So it costs you less to go further. That is the state of airfares today!

Forget about shopping around for a better fare for a few minutes. If you wanted to go to Dallas from New York, you would ordinarily have to pay the full fare of $680. If you wanted to save $280, and you understand this concept, then you would buy a ticket to Oklahoma City instead. This doesn't mean that you have to go there. When you arrive in Dallas - your real destination - you get off the plane as if you were going to change planes, and instead, you keep on going. What you have actually done is purchased a ticket to a "hidden city" for far less than you would otherwise pay.

There are a few disadvantages to this which you should be aware of. First, if you are checking any baggage with the airline, it would have to be checked to Oklahoma City - not where you want it to go. You cannot ask the counter agent to have it sent somewhere else or you would jeopardize your savings. To avoid this, travel light and take all your bags on to the plane with you as carry-on luggage. Your baggage will be subject to the airline's restrictions of one or two carry-on bags.

Second, there might be a problem with your return flight. When the airline discovers that you did not take the second segment of your flight (from Dallas to Oklahoma), they will very likely cancel the reservation you made for your return flight.

There is something you can do about this. You should purchase a one-way ticket. Actually you should purchase two separate one-way tickets - one to go away with and one to get back with. First you will need to determine what the total cost will be. Two one-way tickets normally cost more than a round trip ticket. But two one way tickets to the farther location may cost less than a round trip ticket to your "hidden" destination.

To take advantage of this opportunity you have to do a little homework. First, you will need a copy of the airline's flight schedule from your city to all of its other destinations. You will then have to determine if the city you want to visit is ever used as a hub or as an intermediate stop on longer flights. You do this by looking at the flight numbers used for flights between your starting point and the place you want to go. Then you look at the flight schedule for flights to other cities *beyond* your destination. Then you have to compare the flight numbers for the two destinations to see if there are any similarities. If you see the same flight number, you can probably take advantage of this tactic. Next you have to call the airline's reservation center and ask for rates to each of the two cities. If it is cheaper to go to the second city than to the first, you should reserve for the second city.

This is better illustrated with an example. The cities and flight numbers below are used purely for illustration. Assume that you live in Chicago and want to go to Memphis. Looking at the various airline schedules, you discover that Airline X flies to Memphis. There are 5 flights going there each day; numbers 171, 234, 237, 256 and 259. Further examining the schedule, you find that the airline also flies to New Orleans and that the flight numbers are 201, 234/217, 252, and 256/279. When you see a reference like 234/217, this means that you will first take flight 234 and then change to flight 217. When you see only one flight number, it means this is a direct flight.

Since flight 234 was also listed as a direct flight number to Memphis, you now know that the first segment of the trip to New Orleans would go to Memphis. There you would normally change planes and continue on to New Orleans. Now that you know that Memphis is a "hidden city" on the Chicago to New Orleans flight, you should call the airlines.

Determine the one way fare from Chicago to New Orleans and double that price, since you will be buying two one way tickets. Then call back later and ask the price for a round trip ticket from Chicago to Memphis. If it costs less for the two one way tickets (to and from New Orleans) than it would for the round trip (Chicago to Memphis to Chicago), then you should reserve the flights to New Orleans. Make sure to reserve flights which stop at Memphis on the way.

Using airline hubs and the hidden city routine does not work for every city you may want to go to. It is almost impossible to get to smaller cities this way. If your destination is a major city on either coast - Boston, Washington, D.C., San Francisco or San Diego, you will have difficulty finding one of them as a hidden city. If you are going to a location inland from the coasts and it is a fairly large city, your chances are fairly good of using this trick. Another good bet is if an airline flies from your city to another city more than 4 or 5 times a day. A list of current Hub Cities, as well some of the busier connecting cities used by the major airlines is included in Appendix G. Bear in mind that the airlines often change their patterns, open new hub cities, and reduce traffic to other cities as their business changes.

## Nesting Tickets

To qualify for a Supersaver or other discount fare, airlines often require that you stay over on a Saturday, or that you be away for a minimum of seven days. A practice that has come to be known as "nesting" has developed to overcome these restrictions. The airlines will NOT help you plan this technique. It is sometimes cheaper to purchase two roundtrip Supersaver tickets than to purchase one non-discounted full fare ticket. These discount fares are cheaper because of the number of restrictions involved. Full fares are expensive because there are few, if any, restrictions on them. In many cases, it is not unusual for two plus two to equal three!

As an example, if you wanted to travel from Baltimore to Los Angeles for a short Monday to Thursday trip, you would buy 2 roundtrip Supersaver tickets. The first would be from

Baltimore to Los Angeles departing on Monday, and returning 10-12 days later. The return date is not important as long as it is at least 7 days after the departure date. The second ticket would be from Los Angeles to Baltimore on Thursday, returning to Los Angeles any time after 7 days have elapsed. When you travel from Baltimore, you would use the first coupon of the *first* ticket. When returning from Los Angeles, you use the first coupon of the *second* ticket. At the end of your trip, you can actually throw away the remaining portions and you will generally have saved a substantial amount of money.

Unless there are very heavily discounted rates in effect at the time, you will generally save a substantial amount by buying two roundtrip Supersaver tickets rather than two one ways or one full fare ticket.

Some enterprising people actually squeeze a second trip out of this for no additional cost. If you take a few minutes, you can plan your return dates for each ticket to give you a second free round trip. The second time you travel, you use the second coupon of the second ticket when you go to Los Angeles. Then use the second coupon of the first ticket to travel from Los Angeles back to Baltimore.
This illustration may help you understand this concept better.

### Example of Nesting Airline Tickets

Each ticket you purchase will have 2 coupons (parts).

### Ticket # 1

Coupon # 1 Baltimore to Los Angeles Monday June 5

Coupon # 2 Los Angeles to Baltimore Thursday June 22

### Ticket # 2

Coupon # 1 Los Angeles to Baltimore Thursday June 8

Coupon # 2 Baltimore to Los Angeles Monday June 19

**On the first trip:**

Monday June 5 - use Coupon # 1 of Ticket # 1

Thursday June 8 - use Coupon # 1 of Ticket # 2

**On the second trip:**

Monday June 19 - use Coupon # 2 of Ticket # 2

Thursday June 22 - use Coupon # 2 of Ticket # 1

If you spend enough time planning, you can travel not just for 25% off the full fare, but travel TWICE for the same price! Or you might want to consider placing an ad in the personal section of your newspaper, offering a round trip airline ticket for a bargain price.

# 19

# WHEN A GOOD DEAL MAY BE BAD

If you have followed the advice in this book so far, you will be looking everywhere for travel bargains. It has been suggested that you join the airline and hotel programs and read their literature. You should be reading newspapers, listening to your radio, and watching TV, carefully looking for promotional offers. You should be checking with your travel agent, dealing with coupon brokers and consolidators, and checking with your friends and relatives as well. You should be reading the materials you receive from any travel clubs you decide to join. You have NOT been encouraged to listen for bargains on your telephone. And you have NOT been encouraged to respond to unsolicited bargains which you receive in the mail. There are some offers you should absolutely refuse to become involved with.

One of the biggest disservices the Federal Government can do is to deliver mail from fly-by-night travel firms. Unfortunately, the Postal Service does not know what is contained in mail until it is much too late. Over the last year or two, there have been hundreds of travel scams unmasked. By the time they are discovered by the authorities, they have already packed up and moved on to another address, only to start up under another name. These "boiler rooms" as they have come to be known, have stolen 100's of millions of hard earned dollars from unsuspecting people like you. The New York State Consumer Protection Board recently estimated that more than $100 million was lost in that state alone! The Federal Trade Commission spends a large portion of its budget trying to track these operators down, but has not been very successful.

It is critical that you know how these high pressure firms operate so you can avoid falling victim to their tricks.

Normally you receive a postcard or letter in the mail, advising that you have won a contest or sweepstakes or that you have been chosen for a free vacation. Usually, you receive "Congratulations" of one sort or another. Occasionally, you may be contacted on the telephone by a "travel specialist," who will give you the same story. The postcard almost always indicates that to claim your prize, you have to call a certain number. These are often toll-free numbers. Sometimes you are told to call them collect or that you will be reimbursed for your phone call. Normally, you are told that you only have 24 to 48 hours to respond.

The prize is often a free week at a resort area in a popular place - it's often to the Orlando area. As an additional enticement, you are told that they will also throw in a free cruise if you call within the required time. Sounds too good to be true. Well, it is - too good to be true! What they do not tell you is that the same prize is being offered to thousands of other people like yourself at the very same time.

If you are easily excited about winning a contest, as most people are, you would pick up the phone right away to claim your prize. And you would be congratulated again. To qualify for your prize you might have to join their travel club. Or you might have to purchase a certain number of nights in a hotel. Or you may have to pay half the cost of the hotel. Or you may have to purchase a high priced ticket for the person travelling with you. The cost of these requirements is usually $50-400 or more. At this point, some of them will throw in other bonuses like a cruise (if you didn't originally win it), or a meal at a good restaurant, or a few days of a car rental.

A sure tip-off to a scam is if you are told "today is the last day" to take advantage of the offer. If you hear that, hang up without any further conversation.

If you question their method of operation or whether this is a legitimate offer, or if you otherwise seem suspicious, some of them will actually encourage you to call the Better Business Bureau. And, if you do, you will probably not get a bad report. It takes time for complaints to filter back to the Bureaus. These companies come and go so quickly, there is usually not enough time for complaints to be received.

If you go along with their prize, you will then be asked for your credit card number to speed up processing of your tickets. Or you will be asked to write a check. Some of them will even arrange to have a messenger pick up the check or your cash the next day. Even if you do not go along with their offer, a few of them may ask to verify your credit card number anyway. And you will be charged for their membership dues on your next bill, whether you agreed to it or not.

If you go along with everything up to this point, in a few days you might receive some literature describing your prize. It might not be exactly what was described to you on the phone. Or you might find out that you must request your space in the hotel two or three months in advance and list a number of alternative dates. Or you might be advised that you have to book your reservations through a special company - for a fee, of course. Or that there are additional service charges which will have to be paid in order to claim your prize.

If you patiently wait for your requested dates to be confirmed - and wait - and wait, some day you are going to call the original number back to complain. And you will find out that the phone has been disconnected. They are no longer in business. At least not under the name they used when they contacted you!

Occasionally, you will receive certificates for your vacation. When you get to the hotel, it will be so disgusting that you will be embarrassed to stay in it. Or you will be told that the certificate is only good for 50% of the charges. Or that the certificates are no good at all!

Sometimes, they offer airline tickets at a ridiculously low price, but require you to pay for a number of nights at a luxury hotel. Or it could work the opposite way around - cheap hotel; you pay for the airline. You might make the payment, and take your trip. When you get to the hotel, you might discover that the amount you paid for the room was three times the rate you could have paid if you had simply picked up the phone and called the hotel yourself. When you add up all the charges for the bargain airline tickets and the hotel, you will discover that you may have spent several hundred dollars more than if you had simply paid full price for everything.

Other times you will discover that they used your credit card number and charged mysterious amounts against it. In any event, you will not be happy with your prize, and when it's much too late, you will know that you were a victim of a scam.

There are a number of things you can do to prevent being a victim of one of these operations:

1- Immediately throw away anything received in the mail which sounds similar to what was described above.

2- Hang up immediately on anyone who calls to tell you that you have won a prize - if you have to pay one cent, or if you have to give your credit card number for it.

3- If an offer sounds reasonable, ask for literature to be sent to you. If the offer is legitimate, any reputable business will allow you enough time to study the offer. Be sure to read the fine print very carefully for any restrictions.

4- Question any offer which is free. As the old saying goes - "There's no such thing as a free lunch!" The same goes for free travel; except, of course, for legitimate frequent flyer and frequent guest programs sponsored by reputable companies.

5- If there is any doubt in your mind, call the Better Business Bureau (subject to the warning above), or your State Attorney General's office, or your State Consumer Protection agency. Ask if they have any information about the company which is making the offer to you.

6- If you suspect that you have been a "victim," call the organizations above and seek their help. The Federal Trade Commission, located at 6th and Pennsylvania Ave. N.W., Washington, D.C. 20580 should also be advised. If you use a credit card, you normally have only 60 days after your statement is received to file a dispute. Under certain circumstances, you might receive a credit.

7- Tell yourself that you will say "NO" to any free offer, and instead, settle for saving money the easy way, by using the suggestions in this book.

# 20

# PUTTING
# IT ALL
# TOGETHER

You've covered a lot of territory in the preceding pages. There have been more than a hundred cost saving ideas including the use of consolidators, coupon brokers, frequent flyer programs, affinity cards, couriers, shopping for the best rates and many more. Each of these can help you save money on your next vacation. Make it a point to check each one out. Don't be afraid to make a few phone calls. The people on the other end of the phone deal with people like you every day. You don't have to commit to anything until you are ready.

Be sure to join at least one of the many frequent flyer or frequent guest programs. Try to choose a program which sponsors an affinity credit card. It is really easy to amass points in these programs with one of these cards. Look for creative opportunities to use your card and collect even more points in your program. Watch for special offerings and discount priced sales from your program. These reduced priced sales (fewer points required) are aimed at people who have hundreds of thousands of points in their accounts - but there is nothing to prevent you from taking advantage of them. If you don't receive enough credit for a totally free trip, you should probably have enough for at least an upgrade to First class.

Shop for the best airline, hotel and rental car rates. Learn not to take "No" for an answer ... be persistent. Remember that money saved on airline tickets can be used for a better hotel or even a rental car which you might not have otherwise afforded.

Be sure you find and use a good travel agent. Try to allow for some flexibility in your travel plans. And most important, spend as much time as possible planning. Read as much as you can about your destination. Check your bookstore or local library for books about your destination. Plan what you want to see, where you want to go, and what you want to do when you get there. You deserve a nice vacation. Make it the most memorable one of your life!

Why not extend the length of your vacation? First you might be able to take advantage of better rates. And second, it will give you time to enjoy your vacation even more. We are all interested in *saving* money ... but if you are not able to enjoy *spending* your money, or if you can't take time out to relax and enjoy yourself, then your efforts to find a bargain vacation will have been in vain.

Be sure to go back and read this book again, and take notes as you go along. The more you know about vacations, the easier it will be for you to save money or even Go For Free!

# AFTERWORD

GO FOR FREE! was written out of a sincere desire to help you reduce your annual vacation costs and to share with you the opportunities to receive free vacations. I wanted to provide the most comprehensive guide available on the subject of free and discount travel. In writing it, I have drawn upon my personal travel experiences as well as those of many other frequent travelers.

As mentioned throughout the book, the world of travel is constantly changing. This is an extremely competitive industry. As new travel saving opportunities arise, they will be incorporated into future editions of this book.

I would be interested in hearing from you about your successful vacations and which plans were particularly helpful to you. I would also appreciate any ideas you may have for helping other people save on their trips, and any suggestions you may have for improving future editions. Write to me in care of Ventone Publishing, P.O. Box 100, Merrick, NY 11566.

Although I cannot guarantee your personal success, each money saving plan included has been tried and proven. They work for those who study them and use them.

Start planning your next trip right now. And get ready for a memorable and cost efficient vacation. Good Luck and happy travels!

Dennis P. Sheridan

# APPENDIX A

## MAJOR AIRLINE RESERVATION NUMBERS

| AIRLINE | PHONE NUMBER |
|---|---|
| Aer Lingus | 800-223-6537 |
| Aeroflot | 212-397-1660 |
| Aerolineas Argentinas | 800-327-0276 |
| Aeromexico | 800-237-6639 |
| Aeroperu | 800-255-7378 |
| Air Afrique | 800-237-2747 |
| Air Canada | 800-422-6232 |
| Air France | 800-237-2747 |
| Air India | 800-223-9665 |
| Air Jamaica | 800-523-5585 |
| Air Midwest | 800-835-2953 |
| Air New Zealand | 800-262-1234 |
| Air Panama | 800-272-6262 |
| Alaska | 800-426-0333 |
| ALIA Royal Jordanian | 800-223-0470 |
| Alitalia | 800-442-5860 |
| All Nippon | 800-235-9262 |
| Aloha | 800-367-5250 |
| American | 800-433-7300 |
| America West | 800-247-5692 |
| Austrian | 800-872-4282 |
| Avianca | 800-284-2622 |
| Bahamasair | 800-222-4262 |
| Braniff | 800-272-6433 |
| British Airways | 800-247-9297 |
| BWIA International | 800-327-7401 |
| Canadian Airlines Int'l | 800-426-7000 |
| Cathay Pacific | 800-233-2742 |
| China | 800-227-5118 |
| Comair | 800-354-9822 |
| Continental | 800-525-0280 |
| CSA Czechoslovak | 800-223-2365 |
| Delta | 800-221-1212 |
| Dominicana | 800-662-3737 |
| Eastern | 800-327-8376 |
| Ecuatoriana | 800-328-2367 |
| Egyptair | 800-331-7098 |
| El Al | 800-223-6700 |
| Ethiopian | 800-433-9677 |
| Faucett | 800-334-3356 |
| Finnair | 800-223-5700 |
| Hawaiian | 800-367-5320 |
| Henson | 800-368-5425 |
| Horizon | 800-547-9308 |
| Iberia | 800-772-4642 |
| Icelandair | 800-223-5500 |
| Iraqi Airways | 212-921-8990 |

| | |
|---|---|
| Japan | 800-525-3663 |
| JAT Yugoslav | 800-752-6528 |
| Kenya | 212-832-8810 |
| KLM Royal Dutch | 800-777-5553 |
| Korean | 800-223-1155 |
| Kuwait | 800-424-1128 |
| LACSA | 800-225-2272 |
| Lan Chile | 800-225-5526 |
| LAP Air Paraguay | 800-327-3551 |
| LOT Polish | 800-223-0593 |
| Lufthansa | 800-645-3880 |
| Malaysia | 800-421-8641 |
| Malev Hungarian | 800-223-6884 |
| Mexicana | 800-531-7921 |
| MGM Grand | 800-422-1101 |
| Midway | 800-621-5700 |
| Midwest Express | 800-452-2022 |
| Nigeria | 800-223-1070 |
| Northwest | 800-225-2525 |
| Olympic | 800-223-1226 |
| Pacific Southwest | 800-435-9772 |
| Pakistan | 800-221-2552 |
| Pan Am | 800-221-1111 |
| Phillipine | 800-435-9725 |
| Piedmont | 800-251-5720 |
| Quantas | 800-227-4500 |
| Royal Air Maroc | 800-223-5858 |
| SAA South African | 800-722-4768 |
| SAS Scandanavian | 800-221-2350 |
| Sabena | 800-632-8050 |
| Sahsa Honduras | 800-327-1225 |
| Saudi Arabian | 800-472-8342 |
| Singapore | 800-742-3333 |
| South African | 800-722-9675 |
| Southwest | 800-531-5601 |
| Swissair | 800-221-4750 |
| Taca | 800-535-8780 |
| TAP Air Portugal | 800-221-7370 |
| Thai | 800-426-5204 |
| Tower Air | 800-221-2500 |
| TWA | 800-221-2000 |
| United | 800-241-6522 |
| USAir | 800-428-4322 |
| UTA French | 800-282-4484 |
| Varig | 800-468-2744 |
| Viasa Venezuelan | 800-468-4272 |
| Virgin Atlantic | 800-862-8621 |
| Wardair | 800-237-0314 |

NOTE:Toll free telephone numbers listed are valid from most places within the United States. The number shown may not work in every state or in Canada. Try these numbers first. If you are not successful, call 800-555-1212 for the correct number in your area.

# APPENDIX B

### MAJOR HOTEL/MOTEL RESERVATION NUMBERS

| CHAIN | PHONE NUMBER |
| --- | --- |
| Adam's Mark | 800-231-5858 |
| AMFAC | 800-227-4700 |
| Atlas | 800-854-2608 |
| Best Inns | 800-237-8466 |
| Best Western | 800-528-1234 |
| Budgetel Inns | 800-428-3438 |
| Canadian Pacific | 800-828-7447 |
| Ciga | 800-221-2340 |
| Clarion | 800-252-7466 |
| Comfort Inns | 800-228-5150 |
| Compri | 800-426-6774 |
| Days Inns | 800-325-2525 |
| Delta | 800-268-1133 |
| Doubletree | 800-528-0444 |
| Drury Inns | 800-325-8300 |
| Econo Lodge | 800-446-6900 |
| Economy Motels/Inns | 800-826-0778 |
| El Presidente | 800-433-5456 |
| Embassy Suites | 800-362-2779 |
| Envoy Inns | 800-227-7378 |
| Exel Inns | 800-356-8013 |
| Fairmont | 800-527-4727 |
| Family Inns | 800-251-9752 |
| Fiesta Americana | 800-223-2332 |
| Forte Hotels Int'l | 800-225-3050 |
| Forum | 800-327-0200 |
| Four Seasons | 800-268-6282 |
| Friendship Inns | 800-453-4511 |
| Golden Tulip | 800-344-1212 |
| Guest Quarters | 800-424-2900 |
| Hampton Inns | 800-426-7866 |
| Harley | 800-321-2323 |
| Hawthorn Suites | 800-527-1133 |
| Helmsley | 800-221-4982 |
| Hilton | 800-445-8667 |
| Holiday Inn | 800-465-4329 |
| Howard Johnson's | 800-654-2000 |
| Hyatt | 800-228-9000 |
| Imperial Inns | 800-368-4400 |
| Inter-Continental | 800-332-4246 |
| Jolly | 800-221-2626 |
| L'Ermitage | 800-424-4443 |
| La Quinta | 800-531-5900 |
| Lexington Suites | 800-537-8483 |
| Lincoln | 800-228-0808 |
| Loews | 800-223-0888 |

| | |
|---|---|
| Marriott | 800-228-9290 |
| Master Host | 800-251-1962 |
| Meridien | 800-543-4300 |
| Motel 6   (See Below) | 805-682-6666 |
| Omni/Dunfey | 800-843-6664 |
| Park Suites | 800-432-7272 |
| Penta | 800-225-3456 |
| Pickett Suites | 800-742-5388 |
| Prime Motor Inns | 800-447-7463 |
| Princess | 800-223-1818 |
| Prince | 800-542-8686 |
| Quality Inns | 800-228-5151 |
| Radisson | 800-333-3333 |
| Raintree Inns | 800-824-3662 |
| Ramada Inns | 800-272-6232 |
| Red Carpet Inns | 800-251-1962 |
| Red Lion/Thunderbird | 800-547-8010 |
| Red Roof Inns | 800-848-7878 |
| Regal 8 Inns | 800-851-8888 |
| Regent Int'l | 800-545-4000 |
| Residence Inns | 800-331-3131 |
| Ritz-Carlton | 800-241-3333 |
| Rodeway Inns | 800-228-2000 |
| Romantik | 800-826-0015 |
| Royce | 800-237-6923 |
| Scottish Inns | 800-251-1962 |
| Sheraton | 800-325-3535 |
| Shilo Inns | 800-222-2244 |
| Sonesta | 800-343-7170 |
| Stouffer | 800-468-3571 |
| Super 8 | 800-843-1991 |
| Travelodge/Viscount | 800-255-3050 |
| Treadway Inns | 800-631-0182 |
| Vagabond Inns | 800-522-1555 |
| Wandlyn Inns | 800-561-0006 |
| Westin | 800-228-3000 |
| Westmark | 800-544-0970 |
| Wyndham | 800-822-4200 |

NOTE:Toll free telephone numbers listed are valid from most places within the United States. The number shown may not work in every state or in Canada. Try these numbers first. If you are not successful, call 800-555-1212 for the correct number in your area.

Motel 6 does not provide a toll free telephone number. A copy of the Motel 6 Directory can be obtained by writing to them at 51 Hitchcock Way, Santa Barbara, CA 93105

# APPENDIX C

## U.S. AND CANADIAN AIRLINE FREQUENT FLYER PROGRAMS

| AIRLINE | PROGRAM NAME | PHONE NUMBER | AIRLINE PARTNERS | HOTEL PARTNERS | CAR RENTAL PARTNERS |
|---------|-------------|-------------|------------------|----------------|---------------------|
| Air Canada | Aeroplan | 800-361-8253 | Air ABC<br>Air Alliance<br>Air France<br>Air Ontario<br>Air New Zealand<br>Air Nova<br>Air Toronto<br>Austin Airways<br>Austrian<br>Cathay Pacific<br>Commuter Express<br>First Air<br>Lufthansa<br>Northwest Territorial | CN Hotels<br>Coast Hotels (Canada)<br>Courtyard Inns<br>Hilton Int'l (Canada)<br>Holiday Inns (Canada)<br>Ming Court<br>Prince George (Halifax)<br>Radisson<br>Sheraton<br>Westin<br>West Coast Hotels | Avis<br>Hertz<br>Tilden |
| Alaska | Gold Coast Travel | 800-942-9911 | Hawaiian<br>Horizon Air<br>MarkAir<br>SAS<br>Thai Airways<br>TWA<br>Plus: Holland America Cruise Lines (A) | Red Lion Inns<br>Travellers Inn<br>  (Fairbanks)<br>Westmark Hotels | Budget |
| Aloha | AlohaPass | 800-367-5250 | Aloha IslandAir<br>United (A) | Colony Resorts (A)<br>Sheraton (A) | Budget (A) |
| America West [1] | FlightFund | 800-292-9378 | Singapore (A)<br><br>Plus: Cunard Cruise Lines (A) | Compri<br>Doubletree<br>Marriott | Dollar |

| Airline | Program | Phone | Partner Airlines | Hotels | Car Rentals |
|---|---|---|---|---|---|
| American | AAdvantage | 800-433-7300 | American Eagle, British Airways, Cathay Pacific, Command Airways, Quantas, Singapore, Wings West | Forum, Inter-Continental, Sheraton, Wyndham | Avis, Hertz |
| Braniff | Get-It-All | 800-346-8108 | Air Midwest, Braniff Express, Pan Am (A) | Compri, Doubletree, Hyatt | Budget, National |
| Canadian Airlines International | Canadian Plus | 800-426-7000 | AirAtlantic, Aklak Air, Aloha, Bearskin, British Airways, Burrand Air, CalmAir, KLM, NorcanAir, Nordair Metro, Ontario Express, Pem-Air, Quebecair, Time Air | Canadian Pacific, Delta, Holiday Inns, Marriott, Prince, Pan Pacific | Budget, Thrifty, Tilden |
| Continental AND Eastern | One Pass | 713-952-1630 | Aer Lingus, Air France, Air Micronesia, Air New Orleans, Alitalia, Atlantis, Bar Harbor, Britt Airways, Continental Express, Eastern Express, Iberia, Liat, Lufthansa | Compri, Doubletree, Inter-Continental, Marriott, Radisson, Wyndham | General, National, Thrifty, Tilden |

| Airline | Program | Phone | Airlines | Hotels | Cars |
|---|---|---|---|---|---|
| Continental (continued) | | | Malaysia<br>Metro<br>Precision<br>Provincetown-Boston Airways<br>Rocky Mountain Airways<br>Sabena<br>SAS<br>Southern Jersey<br>Trump Shuttle | | |
| Delta | Frequent Flyer | 800-323-2323 | Air Canada<br>Air New Zealand<br>Atlantic Southeast<br>Business Express<br>Comair<br>Delta Connection<br>Japan Air<br>Lufthansa<br>SkyWest<br>SwissAir | Hyatt<br>Marriott<br>Preferred<br>Trusthouse Forte<br>Viscount | Alamo<br>Avis<br>Hertz<br>National |
| Eastern | See Continental | | | | |
| Hawaiian | Gold Plus | 800-367-5320 | Alaska<br>US Air<br>Tropical | AMFAC | Avis<br>Dollar |
| MGM Grand | Plus Program | 800-422-1101 | | | |
| Midstate [2] | Frequent Flyer Program | 800-826-0522 | | | |
| Midway | Flyers First | 800-621-5700 | Iowa Airways<br>Midway Commuter<br>TWA | Omni Int'l<br>Stouffer | Avis<br>Budget |
| Midwest Express | Frequent Flyer | 800-452-2022 | | | National |

| Airline | Program | Phone | Airlines | Hotels | Car Rentals |
|---|---|---|---|---|---|
| Northwest | Worldperks | 800-435-9696 | Austrian, Big Sky, Express, Mesaba Aviation, Northwest Airlink | Hyatt, Marriott, Radisson | Avis, Budget, National, Thrifty |
| Pan Am | World Pass | 800-348-8000 | Pan Am Express, Pan Am Shuttle | Forum, Inter-Continental, Sheraton | Avis, Dollar, National |
| Piedmont | Frequent Flyer Bonus | 800-722-6687 | Allegheny Commuter, British Airways, Finnair, Hawaiian, Henson, Northwest, Phillipine, Piedmont Commuter, US Air, UTA French, Plus: Carnival Cruise Lines (A) | Marriott, Omni, Radisson, Stouffer | Hertz, National, Tilden |
| Southwest [3] | The Company Club | 800-445-9267 | | | |
| TWA | Frequent Flight Bonus | 800-325-4815 | Air New Zealand, Alaska, Japan, New York Helicopter, Trans World Express | Adam's Mark, Hilton, Marriott | Dollar, Hertz, Thrifty |
| United | Mileage Plus | 800-421-4655 | Air France, Alitalia, Aloha, British Airways, KLM, Lufthansa, SAS, South Central Air, Swissair, United Express, Plus: Holland America Cruise Lines | Hilton, Hyatt, Kempinski, Westin | Alamo, Hertz |

| Airline | Program | Phone | Airline Partners | Hotel Partners | Car Partners |
|---|---|---|---|---|---|
| US Air | Frequent Traveler | 800-872-4738 | Allegheny Commuter<br>British Airways<br>Finnair<br>Hawaiian<br>Henson<br>Lufthansa<br>Northwest<br>Phillipine<br>Piedmont<br>Piedmont Commuter<br>UTA French<br>Plus: Carnival Cruise Lines (A) | Marriott<br>Omni<br>Radisson<br>Stouffer<br>Westin | Hertz<br>National |
| Wardair | Reward | 800-237-0314 | Aloha<br>City Express<br>Thai | | |

**NOTE:** The telephone numbers listed are for the airline frequent flyer program, and not necessarily the same as those used for making reservations. See Appendix A for airline reservation numbers.

Toll free telephone numbers listed are valid from most places within the United States. The number shown may not work in every state or in Canada. Try these numbers first. If you are not successful call 800-555-1212 for the correct number in your area.

FOOTNOTES TO AIRLINE PROGRAM SUMMARY

(A) You do not receive credit in the frequent flyer program for using these companies. The airline awards discounted or free travel with these "partners."

[1]   America West enrolls you at the ticket counter or gate prior to your first flight. Thereafter, you will receive points based on the fare paid.

[2]   Midstate does not require you to join their program in advance. Submit copies of ten tickets and you will receive a corresponding free one-way or roundtrip ticket.

[3]   Southwest enrolls you at the ticket counter or gate prior to your first flight. You will be required to carry a passbook which will be stamped prior to each flight. Fill in the book and earn a free ticket.

# APPENDIX D

FOREIGN AIRLINE FREQUENT FLYER PROGRAMS

| AIRLINE | PROGRAM NAME | PHONE NUMBER |
|---|---|---|
| Air Afrique | Six-For-One | 800-237-2747 |
| AirIndia   [1] | Frequent Traveler Bonus Plan | 800-223-9665 |
| Air Jamaica | Flying Aces | 800-523-5585 |
| All Nippon | GoldPass | 800-235-9262 |
| Avianca   [2] | Avianca Plus | 800-284-2622 |
| China | Bonus Mileage Plan | 800-227-5118 |
| Egyptair   [3] | Bonus Incentive Program | 800-334-6787 |
| El Al   [4] | Matmid | 800-223-6700 |
| Finnair | Frequent Traveler Plan | 800-792-0062 |
| Iberia   [5] | VIP Travel Club | 800-221-9741 |
| Japan   [6] | Mileage Bank | 800-525-6453 |
| Korean | Frequent Traveler Bonus System | 800-223-1155 |
| Lan Chile   [7] | Lan Pass | 800-325-0054 |
| Phillipine   [8] | PALsMILES | 800-435-9725 |
| Quantas   [9] | Frequent Flyer | 800-227-4500 |
| SAA (South African) | Prestige Club | 800-722-4768 |
| Singapore   [10] | Priority Passenger Service | 800-742-3333 |
| TAP Air Portugal | [11] | 800-221-7370 |
| Thai Airways Int'l | Corporate Traveler | 800-426-5211 |
| Virgin Atlantic   [12] | Infrequent Traveler | 800-862-8621 |

NOTE:The telephone numbers listed are for the airline frequent flyer program, and not necessarily the same as those used for making reservations. See Appendix A for airline reservation numbers. The numbers listed are valid from most places within the United States. The number shown may not work in every state or in Canada. Try these numbers first. If you are not successful call 800-555-1212 for the correct number in your area.

FOOTNOTES TO FOREIGN AIRLINE FREQUENT FLYER PROGRAM

[ 1]   Air India gives points for each First or Business class flight, depending on the length of the flight. Ten points are required for the lowest award - a free one-way Business class ticket.

[ 2]   Avianca offers discounted and free Economy and First class trips when you accumulate and submit copies of as few as four prior flight coupons.

[ 3]   Egyptair gives a voucher for all First and Business class flights. These range in value from $250-1000. The vouchers, called Miscellaneous Charge Orders (MCOs), are valid on later travel on the airline of your choice.

[ 4]   The Matmid program has been closed to new memberships since mid-1987 due to its overwhelming popularity. The program may be reopened in the future.

[ 5]   Iberia offers a cash rebate certificate for every flight (including economy) which ranges in value from $75-400 toward future flights on Iberia.

[ 6]   Japan Air Lines credits you for First and Business class flights.It is the only foreign airline in which you can earn credit without leaving the United States. Travel on Delta or TWA may be credited to your JAL account.

[ 7]   Membership in the Lan Chile Lan Pass program requires a $10 fee.

[ 8]   Phillipine gives credit for 20-30% of actual mileage flown in First, Business or full-fare economy. These mileage credits are accumulated and can be used for free travel for up to the number of miles accumulated in your account. 10,000 miles are credited just for signing up.

[ 9]   Quantas requires you to fly at least 70,000 kilometers per year to be eligible for their program.

[10]   Singapore Airlines does not offer a Frequent Flyer program as such.It does offer a special package of benefits to its members,  including free upgrades to First Class. You must fly at least 60,000 miles per year to be eligible.

[11]   TAP Air Portugal does not have a name for its program. It requires you to save copies of your tickets and boarding envelopes. When you submit proof of 5 roundtrips, you receive a coupon for your 6th trip free.

[12]   Virgin Atlantic gives you a voucher good for a free economy trip on a future date each time you fly First class.

# APPENDIX E

## HOTEL FREQUENT GUEST PROGRAMS

| HOTEL | | PROGRAM NAME | PHONE NUMBER | AIRLINE PARTNERS | CAR RENTAL PARTNERS |
|---|---|---|---|---|---|
| Adam's Mark | [ 1] | Gold Mark Club | 800-231-5858 | | |
| Best Western | [ 2] | Gold Crown Club | 800-528-1234 | | |
| Budgetel | [ 3] | Road Runner Club | 800-428-3438 | | |
| Days Inns | [ 4] | Inn-Credible Card Club | 800-344-3636 | | Budget |
| Econolodge | [ 5] | Econo-Traveler's Club | 800-446-6900 | | |
| Fairmont | | President's Club | 800-522-3437 | American | |
| Hilton | [ 6] | HHonors | 800-445-8667 | Eastern TWA United | Hertz National |
| Hilton Int'l | | Vista Club | 800-223-1146 | | |
| Holiday Inns | [ 7] | Priority Club | 800-654-6852 | Pan Am (A) Northwest (A) | Hertz |
| Hyatt | | Gold Passport | 800-544-9288 | Delta Northwest | Hertz |
| Inter-Continental | | Rewards | 800-327-0200 | American Continental Eastern Pan Am | |

Plus: Cunard Line Cruises (A)

| Hotel | | Program | Phone | Airlines | Car Rental |
|---|---|---|---|---|---|
| La Quinta | | CAB Club | 800-531-5900 | | Hertz |
| Marriott | | Honored Guest | 800-228-9290 | Continental Eastern Northwest TWA | Hertz |
| | | | Plus: Norwegian Cruise Lines (A) | | |
| Meridien | | L'invitation | 800-543-4300 | | |
| Omni/Dunfey | | Select Guest | 800-843-6664 | Continental Piedmont US Air | Hertz |
| Radisson | | Key Rewards | 800-333-3333 | Continental Eastern Northwest | Hertz National |
| Ramada | | Business Card | 800-672-6232 | | |
| Red Lion & Thunderbird Inns | [ 8] | Frequent Guest | 800-547-8010 | | Hertz |
| Regal 8 Inns | | Regal Club | 800-851-8888 | | |
| Sheraton | [ 9] | Club International | 800-247-2582 | | |
| Stouffer | [10] | Club Express | 800-468-3571 | Midway Piedmont US Air | Avis |
| Super 8 | | VIP Club | 800-843-1991 | | |
| Travelodge/ Viscount | | Business Break Club | 800-545-6343 | | |
| Treadway | | B.E.S.T | 800-631-0182 | | |
| Vagabond | | 10th Night Free | 800-522-1555 | | |

NOTE: The telephone numbers listed are for the hotel frequent guest program, and not necessarily the same as those used for making reservations. See Appendix B for hotel reservation numbers.

Toll free telephone numbers listed are valid from most places within the United States. The number shown may not work in every state or in Canada. Try these numbers first. If you are not successful call 800-555-1212 for the correct number in your area.

FOOTNOTES TO HOTEL PROGRAM SUMMARY

(A)    You do not receive credit in the frequent guest program for using these companies. The hotel awards discounted or free travel with these "partners."

[ 1]    The Adam's Mark program may be joined prior to registering at the hotel. Generally you must stay about 7 nights before you can take advantage of their benefits.

[ 2]    Best Western offers, in addition to free stays, U.S. Savings Bonds and free membership in AAA. One point is awarded for each dollar spent.

[ 3]    Staying at a Budgetel for twelve nights in a twelve month period entitles you to a free night in their hotel.

[ 4]    The Days Inn program does not offer free nights. Rather it offers a special rate which is at least 10% below the regular rate. They also offer special amenities such as free newspaper etc. Membership also includes no cost group term life insurance and a $25,000 flight coverage plan.

[ 5]    Staying six nights at the same Econolodge property entitles you to one free night at the same hotel.

[ 6]    Hilton prefers that you sign up for their program when you check in at their hotel.

[ 7]    Membership in the Holiday Inns program requires a $10 enrollment fee.

[ 8]    For each stay at a Red Lion, you will receive a coupon good for 5% off a weekday stay or 10% off a weekend stay. These may be accumulated and applied toward a totally free stay.

[ 9]    Sheraton charges an annual fee of $25 for their program. Points earned may be redeemed for free stays, merchandise, or applied toward travel on any major airline, cruise line or car rental company.

[10]    Points earned in Stouffer's program may be redeemed for merchandise, Savings Bonds or free stays.

# APPENDIX F

## AIRLINE AND HOTEL PROGRAMS SPONSORING AFFINITY CREDIT CARDS

| AIRLINE/ HOTEL | PROGRAM NAME | CARD OFFERED | BANK AFFILIATED | ANNUAL RATE | POINTS AWARDED (see below) | BONUS FOR APPLYING | BONUS FOR FIRST USE |
|---|---|---|---|---|---|---|---|
| Alaska | Gold Coast Travel | Visa | Ranier National | 15 | 1 | | |
| America West | FlightFund | Visa | Ranier National | 15 | 2 | | |
| American | AAdvantage | Visa & Master | Citibank | 13.8-16.8 | 1 | 1000 | 400 |
| Canadian | Canadian Plus | Master | Royal Trust | unknown | 1 | 3000 | |
| Continental | One Pass | Master | Marine Midland | varies | 1 | 2500 | 2500 |
| Eastern | One Pass | Master | Marine Midland | varies | 1 | 2500 | 2500 |
| Holiday Inn | Priority Club | Visa | BankOne | 18.96 | 3 | 100 | |
| Marriott | Honored Guest | Visa | FCC National | 16.9 | 4 | | 2000 |
| Northwest | WorldPerks | Visa | BankOne | 17.36 | 1 | 1000 | |
| Pan Am | WorldPass | Master | Lomas | 17.9 | 1 | 1500 | |
| Piedmont | Frequent Flyer Bonus | Visa | North Carolina National | 17.94 | 1 | 2500 | 2500 |
| Ramada | Business Card | Visa | First Tennessee | 16.9 | 5 | 2000 | 1000 |
| Sheraton | Club International | Master | Maryland Bank | 17.9 | 1 | 1000 | |
| TWA | Frequent Flight Bonus | Visa | Chase Manhattan | varies | 1 | | 1000 |
| United | Mileage Plus | Visa | FCC National | 17.9 | 1 | $25 certificate | |
| USAir | Frequent Traveler | Visa | Maryland Bank | 17.9 | 1 | 2000 | |

KEY TO POINTS AWARDED:
1 = One point for each dollar charged
2 = One point (or one dollar credit) for each ten dollars charged
3 = Two points for each ten dollars charged
4 = Three points for each dollar spent at a Marriott. Two points for each dollar spent for other purchases.
5 = Ten points for each dollar spent at a Ramada, plus 50% bonus for using their Visa card.

NOTE: The interest rates noted are subject to change. Many of these banks change the interest rate throughout the year depending upon the current prime rate.

# APPENDIX G

## MAJOR AIRLINE HUB (AND BUSIER) CITIES

| AIRLINE | CITY |
|---|---|
| Alaska | Anchorage |
| | Portland |
| | Seattle |
| American | Chicago |
| | Dallas/Ft. Worth |
| | Nashville |
| | Raleigh/Durham |
| | San Jose |
| America West | Las Vegas |
| | Phoenix |
| Braniff | Dallas |
| | Kansas City |
| | Orlando |
| Continental | Denver |
| | Houston |
| Delta | Atlanta |
| | Dallas/Ft. Worth |
| | Orlando |
| | Salt Lake City |
| Eastern | Atlanta |
| | Philadelphia |
| Midway | Chicago - Midway |
| Northwest | Boston |
| | Detroit |
| | Memphis |
| | Milwaukee |
| | Minneapolis/St. Paul |
| Pan Am | New York (JFK) |
| Piedmont | Charlotte |
| Southwest | Dallas - Love Field |
| | Houston - Hobby |
| | Phoenix |
| TWA | Columbus |
| | St. Louis |
| United | Chicago |
| | Denver |
| USAir | Philadelphia |
| | Pittsburgh |

# APPENDIX H

## CAR RENTAL RESERVATION NUMBERS

| COMPANY | PHONE NUMBER |
|---|---|
| Agency | 800-221-8666 |
| Airways | 800-323-8515 |
| Alamo | 800-327-9633 |
| American Int'l | 800-527-0202 |
| Avis | 800-331-1212 |
| Budget | 800-527-0700 |
| Dollar | 800-421-6868 |
| Enterprise | 800-325-8007 |
| Executive | 800-421-2424 |
| Freedom | 800-331-0777 |
| General | 800-327-7607 |
| Hertz | 800-654-3131 |
| Lindo's | 800-237-8396 |
| Payless | 800-237-2804 |
| Major | 800-346-2567 |
| National | 800-227-7368 |
| Rent A Dent | 800-426-5243 |
| Rent A Wreck | 800-421-7253 |
| RPM | 800-445-4776 |
| Sears | 800-527-0770 |
| Snappy | 800-669-4800 |
| Thrifty | 800-367-2277 |
| Ugly Duckling | 800-843-3825 |
| USA | 800-872-2277 |
| U-Save | 800-272-8728 |
| Value | 800-327-2501 |

NOTE: Toll free telephone numbers listed are valid from most places within the United States. The number shown may not work in every state or in Canada. Try these numbers first. If you are not successful, call 800-555-1212 for the correct number in your area.

# ABOUT THE AUTHOR

Dennis P. Sheridan was employed by Hertz Rent A Car for more than 20 years where, among other things, he was responsible for the development and administration of two different multi-million dollar frequent traveler promotions. He also coordinated efforts with a number of major airlines in setting up partner arrangements for Hertz.

Dennis is an avid traveler and vacationer and has journeyed extensively throughout the United States, Canada and more than 20 countries. Over the last five years, he has taken at least ten vacations, all of them virtually free - using the advice found in this book.

He is a member of most frequent flyer and frequent guest programs, and has attained Gold and Silver status in the American AAdvantage and Eastern One Pass programs respectively.

Presently employed as a Management Consultant, he also conducts travel seminars and is writing a series of other travel related publications in his spare time.

# INDEX

## DID YOU BORROW THIS COPY?

Additional copies of Go For Free! may be obtained by mail from Ventone Publishing. Send a check for $10.95 ($8.95 plus $2 postage and handling) to:

Ventone Publishing
P.O. Box 100
Merrick, NY 11566

Canadian residents: Please add $3.
N.Y. State residents: Please add sales tax.

Allow 4-6 weeks for delivery.

Ventone Publishing also offers a variety of other travel related publications. Write to the address above and request a list of current titles.